*Pocket*
# COPENHAGEN

TOP SIGHTS • LOCAL LIFE • MADE EASY

**Cristian Bonetto**

# In This Book

## QuickStart Guide

Your keys to understanding the city – we help you decide what to do and how to do it

**Need to Know**
Tips for a smooth trip

**Neighbourhoods**
What's where

## Explore Copenhagen

The best things to see and do, neighbourhood by neighbourhood

**Top Sights**
Make the most of your visit

**Local Life**
The insider's city

## The Best of Copenhagen

The city's highlights in handy lists to help you plan

**Best Walks**
See the city on foot

**Copenhagen's Best...**
The best experiences

## Survival Guide

Tips and tricks for a seamless, hassle-free city experience

**Getting Around**
Travel like a local

**Essential Information**
Including where to stay

Our selection of the city's best places to eat, drink and experience:

◎ **Sights**

⊗ **Eating**

😊 **Drinking**

✪ **Entertainment**

🔒 **Shopping**

These symbols give you the vital information for each listing:

| | |
|---|---|
| 📞 Telephone Numbers | 👪 Family-Friendly |
| 🕓 Opening Hours | 🐾 Pet-Friendly |
| P Parking | 🚌 Bus |
| ⊖ Nonsmoking | ⛴ Ferry |
| @ Internet Access | M Metro |
| 📶 Wi-Fi Access | S Subway |
| 🍴 Vegetarian Selection | 🚋 Tram |
| 📖 English-Language Menu | 🚆 Train |

Find each listing quickly on maps for each neighbourhood:

**Bar Hemingway**

16 😊 Map p233, B2

Legend has it that Hemi self, wielding a machine erate this timber-pan ered bar during showpiece is a en by Papa ar town. Dress s.com; Hôtel Rit ⟨ ⊙6.30pm-2a

6 ◎ Plac
Ve

# Lonely Planet's Copenhagen

Lonely Planet Pocket Guides are designed to get you straight to the heart of the city.

Inside you'll find all the must-see sights, plus tips to make your visit to each one really memorable. We've split the city into easy-to-navigate neighbourhoods and provided clear maps so you'll find your way around with ease. Our expert authors have searched out the best of the city: walks, food, nightlife and shopping, to name a few. Because you want to explore, our 'Local Life' pages will take you to some of the most exciting areas to experience the real Copenhagen.

And of course you'll find all the practical tips you need for a smooth trip: itineraries for short visits, how to get around, and how much to tip the guy who serves you a drink at the end of a long day's exploration.

It's your guarantee of a really great experience.

## Our Promise

You can trust our travel information because Lonely Planet authors visit the places we write about, each and every edition. We never accept freebies for positive coverage, so you can rely on us to tell it like it is.

# The Best of Copenhagen 123

## Copenhagen's Best Walks

## Copenhagen's Best ...

# Survival Guide 145

# QuickStart Guide

## Welcome to Copenhagen

Compact Copenhagen is the epitome of Scandi cool. Modernist lamps light New Nordic tables, bridges buzz with cycling commuters, and eye-candy locals dive into pristine waterways. Despite the cobbled streets, whimsical spires and palaces, this is a city at the very cutting edge, bursting at the seams with boundary-pushing food, design and fashion. Go on, take a bite of the (sustainable) good life.

Nyhavn (p58)
CHRIS HEPBURN/GETTY IMAGES ©

# Copenhagen Top Sights

### Tivoli Gardens (p24)

Denmark's number one tourist attraction is also the world's second-oldest amusement park. Slip into a whimsical whirl of story book pavilions, squeal-inducing rides, live music and late-night fireworks, right in the heart of the city.

### Nationalmuseet
(p28)

Relive millennia of Danish history at the engrossing National Museum. This is Denmark's communal attic, jam-packed with prehistoric finds, glittering Viking treasures, astoundingly preserved bodies and retro-fab collectables.

### Christiansborg Slot
(p36)

Seat of the Danish parliament, big, bold Christiansborg Slot is the epicentre of Danish power. It's also a fascinating jumble of history and culture, home to remarkable tapestries, regal carriages, theatre costumes and ancient ruins.

### Designmuseum Danmark (p60)

Drool and swoon at Copenhagen's temple to beautiful design. From Kaare Klint and Hans Wegner to Verner Panton and Arne Jacobsen, the Design Museum's collection is a who's who of visionary Danish style makers.

### Louisiana (p120)

More than just one of Europe's great modern art museums, Louisiana is a soul-stirring experience. Perched by the blue waters of the Øresund, it's a soothing oasis where modernist architecture meets playful garden sculptures and inspiring cultural events.

### Rosenborg Slot (p84)

Ravishing Rosenborg is home to Denmark's dazzling crown jewels, not to mention room after creaky room of regal artefacts, from precious tapestries, timepieces and porcelain to King Christian IV's very own toilet.

## Statens Museum for Kunst (p88)

Copenhagen's National Gallery serves up seven centuries of creativity, including works by Rembrandt, Rubens, Matisse and Munch, not to mention the world's greatest collection of Danish brushstrokes.

## Christiania (p72)

Let your hair down in Europe's most famous commune, a pot-scented microuniverse of DIY abodes and studios, rambling garden paths and free spirits downing beer in the shadow of crumbling barracks.

# Copenhagen Local Life

*Insider tips to help you find the real city*

Beyond Copenhagen's celebrated museums, landmarks and waterfront is the city the locals live and love – a multifaceted place of Nordic market produce, whimsical street art, grit-hip bars and tranquil, romantic gardens.

## Torvehallerne KBH (p90)

▶ Gourmet bites
▶ Artisan produce

Copenhagen's twin-hall food market is a culinary Valhalla, lined with just-plucked Nordic herbs and vegetables, icy seafood, robust meats and cheeses, and local spirits. Stock the pantry or cut straight to the chase and feast on-site at stalls peddling everything from spiced oats, smørrebrød (open sandwiches) and hand-made pasta to craft beers and Third Wave coffee.

## Østerbro (p104)

▶ Heritage architecture
▶ Cosy cafes and eateries

More than just a neigh-bourhood of yummy mummies and yoga mats, posh Østerbro rewards the curious with brightly coloured town houses and story book quarters. There are quiet squares pimped with comfy cafes, and the city's most beautiful, and historic, swimming pool.

## Frederiksberg (p118)

▶ Romantic parks
▶ Subterranean art

Blue-ribbon, bourgeois Frederiksberg delivers an eclectic neighbourhood encounter. It's a place where elegant parks and cosy bistros rub shoulders with fanciful brewery architecture, a zoo and a cistern turned art space.

## Continental Værnedamsvej (p108)

▶ Street life
▶ Food and drink

Live life with a splash of continental flair on compact Værnedamsvej. From organic local liquor and idiosyncratic design to offbeat vintage threads and brilliant brunching, Vesterbro's most cosmo-politan street will leave you humming.

Street art, Christiania (p72)

Coffee Collective (p91), Torvehallerne KBH

### Other great places to experience the city like a local:

# Copenhagen Day Planner

## Day One

Get your bearings with a canal and harbour **tour** (p138), which will have you cruising past some of Copenhagen's most iconic architectural statements, among them **Det Kongelige Bibliotek** (p41). Back on dry land, soak up the salty atmosphere of Nyhavn on your way to 17th-century 'skyscraper' **Rundetårn** (p48). Head to the top for a bird's-eye view of the city.

Make sure to reach **Schønnemann** (p50) before the 1pm lunchtime rush. Your reward is Copenhagen's finest smørrebrød (open sandwiches), best washed down with bracing akvavit. Afterwards, take a stroll through the Latin Quarter, dropping in on Bertel Thorvaldsen's Christ and 12 apostles inside **Vor Frue Kirke** (p48). From here, stroll across to **Nationalmuseet** (p28), where you can spend a few hours exploring Denmark's past.

From here, it's a quick walk to the well-seasoned charm of **Tivoli Gardens** (p24), the world's second-oldest amusement park. Dine at historic **Grøften** (p33), then hit the rides, catch a concert or simply soak up Tivoli's old-fashioned story-book vibe.

## Day Two

After breakfast at **Atelier September** (p96), walk in royal footsteps at Renaissance **Rosenborg Slot** (p84), home to the Danish crown jewels. Adjacent is **Kongens** (p87) Have, one of the city's best-loved parks. If you need a caffeine fix, take a pit stop at **Forloren Espresso** (p67), then eye-up art and antiques as you saunter up Bredgade to glorious **Marmorkirken** (p64).

Close by lies **Designmuseum Danmark** (p60). If you're peckish, lunch at the museum cafe before exploring its fetching collection of applied arts, both Danish and foreign. When done, drop in on the royals at their inner-city abode, **Amalienborg Slot** (p64). The palace sits beside the harbour, from where you can debate the architectural merits of the divisive **Operaen** (p80).

If you didn't manage to secure a table at **Noma** (p78), you will have booked a table at fellow New Nordic star **Kadeau** (p78) or **Kanalen** (p78); all three are located on Christianshavn. Taste buds thrilled, continue the night with elegant wine and conversation at **Ved Stranden 10** (p52), innovative cocktails at **Ruby** (p52), and maybe a little late-night sax at **La Fontaine** (p54).

**Short on time?**
We've arranged Copenhagen's must-sees into these day-by-day itineraries to make sure you see the very best of the city in the time you have available.

## Day Three

☀ If you have a third day, escape the city with a trip to **Louisiana** (p121), an easy train ride north of central Copenhagen. Get up close and personal to works by international greats like Bacon, Picasso and Warhol, as well as home-grown cultural deities such as Asger Jorn. Amble through its sculpture-studded grounds and stay for lunch.

☀ Back in the city, spend the afternoon exploring the self-proclaimed autonomous neighbourhood **Christiania** (p72). Get off its infamous main drag – dubiously dubbed Pusher St – and take in the commune's fascinating organic architecture, snug gardens and handful of craft studios. If the weather is in a good mood, grab a beer and join your fellow free spirits for a sip in the sun.

☾ As evening descends, trade hippy for hip in Vesterbro's Kødbyen (Meat City), a meatpacking district turned buzzing restaurant, bar and gallery hub. Opt for superlative seafood at **Kødbyens Fiskebar** (p113), Euro-fusion at **Paté Paté** (p115), or go carnivorous at **Nose2Tail** (p115). If the night is still young, dive into **Mesteren & Lærlingen** (p117) or nearby **Bakken** (p116).

## Day Four

☀ Kick-start your day with an organic pastry to go from **Meyers Bageri** (p66), before delving into Danish and European masterpieces at **Statens Museum for Kunst** (p88). Alternatively, explore the extraordinary collection of art at **Ny Carlsberg Glyptotek** (p31) or lesser-trampled **Davids Samling** (p93).

☀ Appetite piqued, dive into the gastronomic wonderland of **Torvehallerne KBH** (p90), the city's celebrated food market. Grab a seat at one of the many food stalls for a whisker-licking bite, then scour stalls packed with fresh produce, pungent cheeses and artisan pantry fillers. Cross the nearby lakes into grungy Nørrebro, home to tranquil **Assistens Kirkegård** (p101) and super-cool shopping and eating strip Jægersborggade.

☾ Jægersborggade is home to **Manfreds og Vin** (p101), a locavore-minded eatery where regional produce, interesting wines and an easy vibe fuse to satisfying effect. Keep the night rolling with dirt-cheap cocktails at **Kassen** (p103) or sultry tunes at **Kind of Blue** (p102), or hit the dance floor at Nørrebro classic **Rust** (p103).

# Need to Know

**For more information,
see Survival Guide (p146)**

## Currency
Danish krone (Dkr)

## Language
Danish; English widely spoken

## Visas
No entry visa is required for citizens of EU and Scandinavian countries, or for citizens of the USA, Canada, Australia and New Zealand for stays of up to three months. Nationalities requiring a visa are listed at www.nyidanmark.dk.

## Money
ATMs widely available and credit cards accepted at most hotels, stops and restaurants. Foreign credit cards often incur a fee of up to 3.75%.

## Mobile Phones
Local SIM cards widely available for use in most international mobile phones. Mobile coverage widespread.

## Time
Central European Time (GMT/UTC plus one hour)

## Plugs & Adaptors
Standard continental (European) plug of two round prongs; current is 220V.

## Tipping
Largely unexpected and unnecessary, though a small tip (around 10%) is not uncommon in higher-end restaurants with very good service.

## ① Before You Go

### Your Daily Budget

#### Budget less than Dkr800
▶ Double room in budget hotel Dkr500–650
▶ Cheap meals under Dkr125
▶ 24/72-hour City Pass for Copenhagen transport Dkr80/200

#### Midrange Dkr800–1500
▶ Double room in midrange hotel Dkr700–1500
▶ Museum admission Dkr50–110
▶ Three-course menu Dkr300

#### Top end more than Dkr1500
▶ Double room in top-end hotel from Dkr1500
▶ New Nordic degustation menu from Dkr700

### Useful Websites
▶ **Lonely Planet** (www.lonelyplanet.com/copenhagen) Destination low-down, hotel bookings, reviews and forums.

▶ **Visit Copenhagen** (www.visitcopenhagen.com) Copenhagen's official tourism website.

▶ **Rejseplanen** (www.rejseplanen.dk) Handy journey planner.

### Advance Planning
▶ **Two months before** Book your hotel – prices increase the closer you get to your arrival date – and (try) to score a table at Noma.

▶ **Three weeks before** Secure a table at hot-spot restaurants like Kadeau.

▶ **One week before** Scan www.visitcopenhagen.com and www.aok.dk for upcoming events.

## 2 Arriving in Copenhagen

**Copenhagen Airport** (www.cph.dk) is located in Kastrup, 9km southeast of central Copenhagen. Easy, around-the-clock connections to the city via train and metro cost about Dkr36. A taxi ride is Dkr250 to Dkr300.

Cruise ferries to and from Norway dock at Søndre Frihavn, located 2km north of Kongens Nytorv. Bus 26 connects the port to the city centre and Vesterbro.

### ✈ From Copenhagen Airport (CPH)

| Destination | Best Transport |
| --- | --- |
| Tivoli | train to Central Station |
| Slotsholmen | metro to Christianshavn or train to Central Station |
| Strøget & Around | metro to Kongens Nytorv or train to Central Station |
| Nyhavn | metro to Kongens Nytorv |
| Christianshavn | metro to Christianshavn |
| Nørreport | metro or train to Nørreport |
| Vesterbro | train to Central Station |

### 🚢 From Søndre Frihavn

| Destination | Best Transport |
| --- | --- |
| Tivoli | train to Central Station |
| Slotsholmen | bus 26 |
| Strøget & Around | bus 26 |
| Nyhavn | bus 26 |
| Christianshavn | bus 26 to Kongens Nytorv, then metro to Christianshavn |
| Nørreport | train to Nørreport |
| Vesterbro | bus 26 |

## 3 Getting Around

Copenhagen has an extensive public transit system consisting of a metro, train, bus and ferry network.

### 🚌 Bus

Extensive coverage, with seven primary routes, each with the letter 'A' in the route number. These routes run every three to seven minutes in peak hour, and about every 10 minutes at other times. Night buses (denoted by an 'N' in the route number) run on a few major routes between 1am and 5am nightly.

### Ⓜ Metro

Two lines, M1 and M2. Services run around the clock: every two to four minutes in peak times, three to six minutes during the day and on weekends, and seven to 20 minutes at night. Both lines connect Nørreport with Kongens Nytorv and Christianshavn. Line M2 (yellow line) runs to the airport.

### 🚆 S-Train (S-Tog)

Suburban train network running seven lines through Central Station (Københavns Hovedbanegård). Services every four to 20 minutes, 5am to 12.30am. All-night services hourly on Friday and Saturday (half-hourly on line F).

### 🚢 Harbour Bus

The city's commuter ferries are known as Harbour Buses. There are three routes, servicing 10 stops along the harbourfront.

### 🚲 Bicycle

Most streets have cycle lanes and, more importantly, motorists tend to respect them. Bikes can be carried free on S-trains, but are prohibited at Nørreport station during weekday peak hours. Bikes can be carried on the metro, except during peak hours, September to May.

# Copenhagen Neighbourhoods

**Worth a Trip**
**⊙ Top Sights**
Louisiana

**Nørrebro (p98)**
Copenhagen at its graffiti-scrawled best, jam-packed with indie cafes and rocking bars, retro treasures and buried Danish legends.

**Tivoli Area (p22)**
Copenhagen's bustling 'welcome mat', home to the cultural blockbuster Nationalmuseet and ageless charmer Tivoli Gardens.

**⊙ Top Sights**

Tivoli Gardens

Nationalmuseet

**Vesterbro (p106)**
The pinnacle of Copenhagen cool, where postindustrial bars, eateries and galleries mix it with vintage thrift shops and the odd porn peddler.

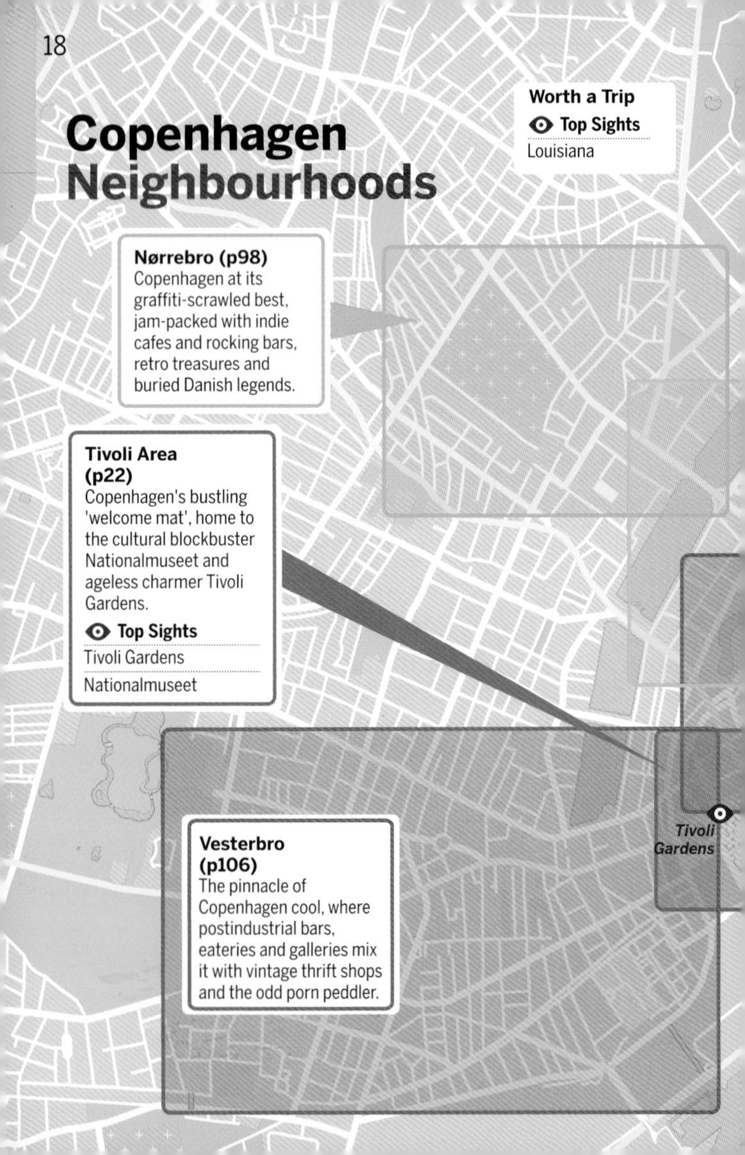

⊙ *Tivoli Gardens*

## Nørreport
### (p82)

An appetite-piquing, soul-stirring feast of market produce, artistic masterpieces, royal turrets and jewels, and dashing parklands.

**⊙ Top Sights**

Rosenborg Slot

Statens Museum for Kunst

## Strøget & Around
### (p44)

Nordic fashion flagships, buzzing cafes and bars, and twisting cobbled streets draw the crowds in Copenhagen's historic heart.

## Nyhavn & the Royal Quarter (p58)

Masts and maritime buildings, a rococo royal palace and the world's most famous mermaid – welcome to the city of postcard images.

**⊙ Top Sights**

Designmuseum Danmark

## Christianshavn
### (p70)

Scandinavia's answer to Amsterdam, pimped with cosy canals, boats and cafes, and the pot-scented streets of alt-living commune Christiania.

**⊙ Top Sights**

Christiania

*Statens Museum for Kunst* ⊙

*Designmuseum Danmark* ⊙

*Rosenborg Slot* ⊙

*Christiansborg Slot* ⊙

⊙ *Nationalmuseet*

⊙ *Christiania*

## Slotsholmen
### (p34)

Parliamentary palace, medieval ruins, blue-blooded artefacts and a gobsmacking library: tiny Slotsholmen packs a powerful punch.

**⊙ Top Sights**

Christiansborg Slot

# Explore
# **Copenhagen**

Christiansborg Slot (p36)
NICO STENGERT/NA/NOVARC/CORBIS ©

Explore

# Tivoli Area

The Tivoli area is Copenhagen's punchy introduction. It's here that you'll find Central Station (Københavns Hovedbanegård), the Copenhagen Visitors Centre, and cultural heavyweight, Nationalmuseet. From Rådhus to Ny Carlsberg Glyptotek, iconic architecture punctuates the skyline. Last but not least is Denmark's star attraction, Tivoli Gardens, an amusement park with more charm than Cary Grant.

## The Sights in a Day

☀ If you're freshly arrived, drop in at the **Copenhagen Visitors Centre** (p151), which offers free wi-fi and a free city map with bus routes. Soaring across the street is the landmark Radisson Blu Royal Hotel. Designed by architectural deity Arne Jacobsen, it was the city's first skyscraper when completed in 1960. From here it's an easy walk to the whimsical **Rådhus** (p31), Copenhagen's fantastical city hall.

☼ Another quick walk leads you to Denmark's pre-eminent cultural institution, **Nationalmuseet** (p28). Spend a few hours nosing through its millennia-spanning collection and grab a bite at the in-house cafe. Alternatively, lunch in the Winter Garden at **Ny Carlsberg Glyptotek** (p31) before taking in one of Denmark's finest collections of impressionist art and classical antiquities.

☾ Done, ditch art for adrenaline across the street at **Tivoli Gardens** (p24). Dine the old-school way at **Grøften** (p33), one of Tivoli's plethora of eateries. If it's Friday night, consider catching Tivoli's free summer-season rock concert. Alternatively, snuggle up with a crafty libation at grown-up **Nimb Bar** (p33).

### ◉ Top Sights

Tivoli Gardens (p24)

Nationalmuseet (p28)

### ♥ Best of Copenhagen

**Museums & Galleries**
Nationalmuseet (p28)

Ny Carlsberg Glyptotek (p31)

**Hygge**
Tivoli Gardens (p24)

**For Kids**
Tivoli Gardens (p24)

Nationalmuseet (p28)

### Getting There

🚇 **S-Train** S-trains service both Central Station (Københavns Hovedbanegård) and Vesterport station to the northwest of it. Trains to and from Copenhagen Airport also run to Central Station.

🚌 **Bus** Rådhuspladsen is the main hub for city buses. Routes 2A, 5A, 9A, 11A, 30, 40, 66 and 250S stop directly in front of Central Station and Tivoli Gardens. The area is compact, so once you're here, explore it on foot.

## Top Sights
# Tivoli Gardens

Unleash your inner child at Tivoli Gardens. The country's top-ranking tourist draw, this veteran amusement park and pleasure garden has been eliciting gleeful shrills since 1843. It's the world's second-oldest amusement park, and one that inspired none other than Walt Disney. Generations on, the place continues to win fans with its dreamscape of rides, exotic pavilions, open-air stage shows and laser shows. Whatever your idea of fun – gut-wrenching roller-coaster rides, romantic carousels or alfresco pantomime and beer – this old-timer has you covered.

👁 Map p18, B2

www.tivoli.dk

adult/child under 8yr Dkr99/free

🕑 11am-10pm Sun-Thu, 11am-12.30am Fri, 11am-midnight Sat Apr-Sep, reduced hours rest of year

🚌 2A, 5A, 9A, 12, 26, 250S, 350S, 🚉 S-train København H

Carousel, Tivoli Gardens

# Don't Miss

### Star Flyer

One of the world's tallest carousels, the Star Flyer will have you whizzing round and round at heights of up to 80m. It's a bit like being on a sky-scraping swing, travelling at 70km/h and taking in a breathtaking view of Copenhagen's historical towers and rooftops. The astrological symbols, quadrants and planets on the ride are a tribute of sorts to Danish astronomer Tycho Brahe.

### Roller Coasters

Rutschebanen (The Roller Coaster) is the best loved of Tivoli's roller coasters, rollicking its way through and around a faux 'mountain' and reaching speeds of 60km/h. Built in 1914 it claims to be the world's oldest operating wooden roller coaster. If you're hankering for something a little more hardcore, jump on the Dæmonen (The Demon), a 21st-century beast with faster speeds and a trio of hair-raising loops.

### Aquila

Like the Star Flyer, Aquila (Eagle) is also a nod to the country's most famous astronomer, the ride named for the constellation which Brahe observed through his 16th-century telescope. The ride itself is a breathtaking, gut-wrenching swing and spinner ride, with centrifugal powers up to 4G that will have you spinning around and upside down. If you enjoy viewing the world from a different angle, this one's for you.

### The Grounds

Beyond the roller coasters, carousels and side stalls is a Tivoli of beautifully landscaped gardens, tranquil nooks and eclectic architecture. Lower the adrenaline under beautiful old chestnut and elm trees, and amble around Tivoli

## ☑ Top Tips

▸ Amusement ride tickets cost Dkr25 (some rides require up to three tickets), making the multiride ticket (Dkr199) better value in most cases.

▸ Tivoli is at its most enchanting in the evening, when the park's fairy lights and lanterns take the enchantment to a whole new level.

▸ Although the free Friday music concerts (summer season only) commence at 10pm, head in by 8pm if it's a big-name act or risk missing out.

## ✕ Take a Break

Tivoli is packed with food and beverage outlets, serving everything from hot dogs and beer to global fare. It's most famous restaurant is Grøften (p33), a veritable institution.

Lake, gently rippling with koi carps, goldfish and ducks. Formed out of the old city moat, the lake is a top spot to snap pictures of Tivoli's commanding Chinese Tower, built in 1900. The lake itself is also home to the swashbuckling St George III, an 18th-century frigate turned restaurant.

### Illuminations & Fireworks

Throughout the summer season, Tivoli Lake wows the crowds with its nightly laser and water spectacular. While it mightn't match the scale of similar shows in cities like Dubai and Las Vegas, its combination of lasers, shooting water and an orchestral score are still a hit, especially with kids. Another summer-season must are the Saturday evening fireworks, repeated again from December 26 to 30 for Tivoli's annual Fireworks Festival. Check the website for all times and details.

### Live Performances

Tivoli delivers a jam-packed program of live music. The indoor Tivolis Koncertsal (Concert Hall) hosts mainly classical music, with the odd musical and big-name pop or rock act. Outdoor stage Plænen is the venue for Fredagsrock, Tivoli's free, hugely popular Friday evening concerts. Running from early April to mid-September, the acts span numerous genres, from pop, rock and neofolk to hip hop, jazz and funk (recent acts include the UK's Simple Minds and Passenger). All tickets are sold at the Tivoli Billetcenter or online through the Tivoli website.

### Christmas Festivities

Even the toughest scrooges melt at the sight of Tivoli in November and December, when the entire park turns into a Yuletide winter wonderland (cue live reindeer and special Christmas rides). The Tivoli Christmas market is one of the city's best-loved traditions, heady with the scent of cookies, pancakes and *gløgg* (mulled wine). It's also a good spot to pick up those nifty Nordic handicrafts.

### Pantomime Theatre

Tivoli's criminally charming Pantomime Theatre debuted in 1874. It's the work of prolific architect Vilhelm Dahlerup, responsible for many of Copenhagen's most iconic buildings, including the Ny Carlsberg Glyptotek and Statens Museum for Kunst. Dahlerup's historicist style shines bright in his Tivoli creation, a colour-bursting ode to the Far East. Each night during the summer season, the silent stage presents plays in the tradition of Italy's Commedia dell'Arte. Many of the performers also work at the esteemed Royal Ballet. See the Tivoli website for details.

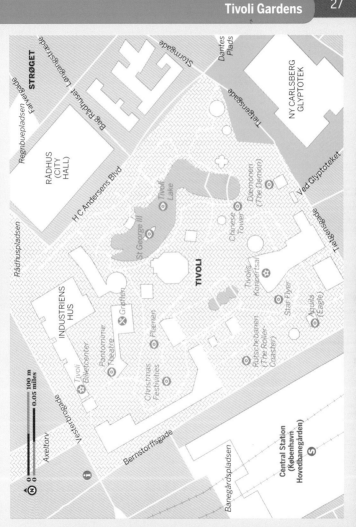

## Top Sights
# Nationalmuseet

Like a multilevel time machine, Copenhagen's National Museum hurls visitors through Denmark's eventful past. The museum has first claim on virtually every antiquity found in Denmark, and its hefty hoard includes Stone Age tools, Viking-era rune stones and jewellery, and 18th-century fashions and interiors. It's here that you'll find the country's fabled Sun Chariot, not to mention the ill-fated Iron Age Huldremose Woman. Beyond these Danish icons is an eclectic mix of foreign acquisitions, including classical coins and Central Asian costumes.

◉ Map p18; E3

www.natmus.dk

Ny Vestergade 10

admission free

◷ 10am-5pm Tue-Sun

🚌 1A, 2A, 11A, 33, 40, 66,
🚉 S-train København H

Nationalmuseet

# Don't Miss

### Danish Prehistory Collection

You'll find many of the museum's most spectacular finds in the Prehistory Collection. Among these is a finely crafted 3500-year-old Sun Chariot, unearthed in a Zealand field, and the spectacular Gundestrup cauldron, Europe's oldest example of Iron Age silverwork. Even more astounding is the Huldremose Woman, an extraordinarily well-preserved Iron Age time traveller still wrapped in her cloaks.

### Stories of Denmark 1660–2000

Upstairs, the *Stories of Denmark: 1660–2000* exhibition traces Denmark's evolution from absolute monarchy to modern nation in three chronological sections: Under the Absolute Monarchy 1660–1848, People and Nation 1848–1915, and Welfare State 1915–2000. Its 37 rooms heave with a staggering array of public and personal artefacts, from weaponry and armour to portraits, crockery and folk costumes.

### People of the Earth

The National Museum's ethnographic collection covers everything from African masks and Indian temple sculptures to ornate cloaks and saddle bags from the Pamir region of Central Asia. A small but notable collection of objects from the Arctic region includes an extraordinary child's fur from Canada, fastened with 80 amulets, including fox teeth and a herring gull's foot. Such adornments were believed to ward off evil and lure good fortune.

☑ **Top Tips**

▶ On Saturdays in June, August and September, the museum runs guided tours (Dkr50) of a well-preserved Victorian-era apartment, just a few metres from the museum. Tours (in English) commence at 2pm. Register at the museum information desk.

▶ If you're visiting with kids, let them loose in the Children's Museum, where they can play dress-ups and role-play in a variety of recreated historical settings.

✗ **Take a Break**

The museum's restaurant and cafe are handy spots for an in-house bite or coffee. For a postmuseum drink, it's only a 750m walk to outstanding Ved Stranden 10 (p52).

IMAGE PROVIDER/ALAMY ©

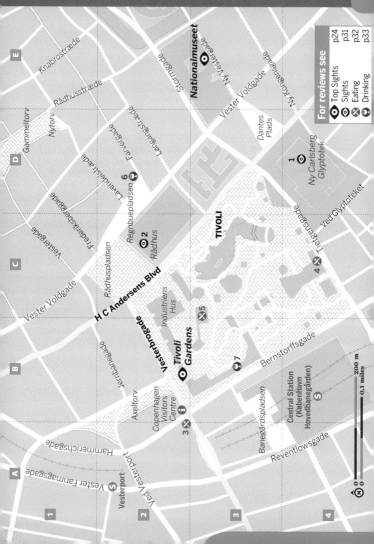

Rådhus

# Sights

## Ny Carlsberg Glyptotek  MUSEUM

1 ◉ Map p30, D4

Fin-de-siècle architecture dallies with an eclectic mix of art at Ny Carlsberg Glyptotek. The collection is divided into two parts: Northern Europe's largest booty of antiquities, and an elegant collection of 19th-century Danish and French art. The latter includes the largest collection of Rodin sculptures outside of France, and no less than 47 Gauguin paintings. These are displayed along with works by greats like Cézanne, Van Gogh, Pissarro, Monet and Renoir. (www.glyptoteket.dk; Dantes Plads 7, HC Andersens Blvd; adult/child Dkr75/free, Sun free; ☺11am-5pm Tue-Sun; ☐1A, 2A, 11A, 33, 40, 66, ⦿S-train København H)

## Rådhus  HISTORIC BUILDING

2 ◉ Map p30, C2

Completed in 1905, Copenhagen's National Romantic–style town hall is the work of architect Martin Nyrop. The building's most famous resident is the curious **Jens Olsen's World Clock** (admission free; ☺9am-5pm Mon-Fri, 10am-1pm Sat), designed by astromechanic Jens Olsen (1872–1945) and built at a cost of 1 million kroner. Not only does it display local time, but also solar time, sidereal time, sunrises and sunsets, firmament and celestial pole migration, planet revolutions, the Gregorian calendar and even changing holidays! You can also climb the 105m city hall **tower** (admission Dkr20; ⏱tours 11am & 2pm Mon-Fri, noon Sat, min 4 people) for a commanding view of the city. (City Hall; admission free; ⏱7.45am-5pm Mon-Fri, 10am-1pm Sat; 🚌1A, 2A, 11A, 12, 26, 33, 40, 66, 🚆S-train København H)

☑ Top Tip

**Bike Safety**

Knowing some of the local rules and customs will help you bike more safely:

▶ Keep right unless overtaking another cyclist

▶ Don't cycle on footpaths or pedestrianised streets

▶ Walk your bicycle across crosswalks

▶ Do not turn right on a red light

▶ Give way to bus passengers crossing bike lanes

▶ Lock your bike – bike theft occurs

▶ Signal right (right arm out and low) before turning right, signal left (left arm out and low) before turning left, and use the stop signal (left hand up) when making an atypical stop on the cycle path, or if stopping to turn left at a main intersection

# Eating

## Alberto K                    MODERN DANISH $$$

3 🍴  Map p30, A2

Perched on the 20th floor of the Radisson Blu Royal Hotel, Alberto K is a culinary high, both literally and metaphorically. Award-winning head chef Jeppe Foldager marries modern French techniques with local produce from small producers, creating arresting dishes that are vibrant and seductive. Arne Jacobsen cutlery and furniture pay tribute to the hotel's celebrated designer, while the restaurant's wine cellar is an oenophile's delight. (📞33 42 61 61; www.alberto-k.dk; Hammerichsgade 1; 5/7 courses Dkr750/950; ⏱6-9.45pm Mon-Sat; 🚌5A, 6A, 26, 🚆S-train Vesterport, København H)

## Wagamama                    JAPANESE $$

4 🍴  Map p30, C4

Yes, it's a ubiquitous UK chain, but we still love Wagamama for several reasons: the food is fresh and flavoursome, the place is open all week, and it's a short walk from Central Station. Pique the appetite with tasty gyoza or vibrant seaweed salad, then slurp your way through steamy bowls of ramen noodles. (www.wagamama.dk; Tietgensgade 20; mains Dkr95-135; ⏱noon-9pm daily; 🛜; 🚌1A, 2A, 5A, 9A, 11A, 🚆S-train København H)

## Grøften
DANISH $$

5 ✕ Map p30, C3

If you're getting your thrills at Tivoli, jolly Grøften is a handy place to refuel. Sure it's a bit touristy, but it's been here since 1874, making it a bit of a local institution. Reminisce about the good old days over smørrebrød (open sandwich) classics like hand-peeled shrimps with lemon and mayonnaise, or tackle the mains, which includes gutsy, no-nonsense meat and fish dishes. (☎33 75 06 75; www.groeften.dk; smørrebrød Dkr69-135, mains Dkr145-385; ⊙noon-10pm daily Apr-Sep, reduced hours rest of year; ☎; ☐2A, 5A, 9A, 97N, 250S, ☒S-train København H)

# Drinking

## Oscar Bar & Cafe
GAY

6 ⬤ Map p30, D2

In the shadow of Rådhus, this corner cafe-bar remains the most popular gay in the village. There's food for the peckish and a healthy quota of eye-candy locals and out-of-towners. In the warmer months, its alfresco tables are packed with revellers, one eye on friends, the other on Grindr. (www.oscarbarcafe.dk; Regnbuepladsen 77; ⊙11am-11pm Sun-Thu, to 2am Fri & Sat; ☎; ☐12, 26, 33, 11A, ☒S-train København H)

## Gender Equality

Denmark is one of the world's most gender-equal societies, ranking number eight internationally in the World Economic Forum's 2013 gender gap index. The country ranked first for educational attainment, 11th for political empowerment and 25th for economic participation and opportunity. Women students outnumber men at tertiary level, while figures released by the OECD (Organisation for Economic Co-operation and Development) in 2013 showed that the average Danish man undertakes 47% of all domestic chores.

## Nimb Bar
COCKTAIL BAR

7 ⬤ Map p30, B3

If you fancy chandeliers, quirky murals and an open fire with your well-mixed drink, make sure this ballroom bar is on your list. Located inside super-chic Hotel Nimb, it was kick-started by legendary bartender Angus Winchester. The beer is expensive, but you're here for seasonal, classically styled cocktails. Period. (☎88 70 00 00; www.tivoli.dk/nimb; Bernstorffsgade 5; ⊙5pm-midnight Sun-Thu, to 1am Fri & Sat; ☐2A, 5A, 9A, 250S, ☒S-train København H)

Explore

# Slotsholmen

It might be small, but the 'island' of Slotsholmen has played a leading role in Copenhagen's history. It was here that Bishop Absalon founded a fortress in 1167, and it was around this fortress that Denmark's future capital city began to grow. The main protagonist is mighty Christiansborg Slot, home to the national parliament and to a string of cultural attractions.

# The Sights in a Day

☀ If you're a fan of historic theatres, consider starting at the **Teatermuseet** (p38). Alternatively, eye up the chiselled beauties of Denmark's most revered sculptor at **Thorvaldsens Museum** (p41) or schmooze with sculpted royals and common folk at **Kongernes Lapidarium** (p42), set in a Renaissance brewery.

☀ Across the street from Kongernes Lapidarium is **Det Kongelige Bibliotek** (Royal Library; p41), whose 'Black Diamond' extension is one of Copenhagen's most fetching examples of contemporary architecture. If you're on a tight budget, lunch at **Øieblikket** (p43). If not, settle in at **Søren K** (p43). Both are located inside the library.

🌙 Head back to Christiansborg Slot, buy a combination ticket, and spend the afternoon exploring the palace's ancient ruins, Royal Reception Chambers and Royal Stables. It will cost you nothing to climb the palace's lofty tower, which offers a commanding view of Denmark's handsome capital. Alternatively, spend the afternoon learning about Denmark's Jewish heritage at the **Dansk Jødisk Museum** (p42).

## 👁 Top Sights
Christiansborg Slot (p36)

## 💜 Best of Copenhagen
**Museums**
Thorvaldsens Museum (p41)

Kongernes Lapidarium (p42)

Dansk Jødisk Museum (p42)

Tøjhusmuseet (p42)

**Architecture**
Christiansborg Slot (p36)

Det Kongelige Bibliotek (p41)

Børsen (p43)

## Getting There

🚌 **Bus** Slotsholmen is well serviced by bus, with routes 1A, 2A, 9A, 26, 40 and 66 all running across the island. Slotsholmen itself is easily navigable on foot.

Ⓜ **Metro** The closest metro station is Christianshavn, 400m east of Slotsholmen.

⚓ **Harbour Bus** Commuter ferries stop at the southern tip of the island, just beside Det Kongelige Bibliotek.

## Top Sights
# Christiansborg Slot

Fans of the internationally acclaimed Danish political drama *Borgen* will know it as the workplace of dashing *statsminister* (prime minister) Birgitte Nyborg. Others will simply know it as that vast, slightly foreboding palace in the heart of the city. The building in question is Christiansborg Slot. This is the nation's power base, home to the Danish Folketinget (parliament), Prime Minister's office and Supreme Court. It's also home to an eclectic array of cultural draws from ruins and tapestries to Cinderella carriages.

⊙ Map p18; C2

☎ 33 92 64 92

www.christiansborg.dk

🚌 1A, 2A, 9A, 26, 40, 66,
🚏 Det Kongelige Bibliotek,
Ⓜ Christianshavn

# Don't Miss

### Royal Reception Rooms

The grandest part of Christiansborg is **De Kongelige Repræsentationslokaler** (Map p40, B2; Royal Reception Rooms; www.ses.dk; adult/child Dkr80/40; ☺10am-5pm daily May-Sep, closed Mon rest of year, guided tours in Danish 11am, in English 3pm), an ornate Renaissance hall where the queen holds royal banquets and entertains heads of state. Of particular note are the riotously colourful wall tapestries depicting Danish history from Viking times to today. Created by tapestry designer Bjørn Nørgaard over a decade, the works were completed in 2000. Keep an eye out for the Adam and Eve–style representation of the queen and her husband (albeit clothed) in a Danish Garden of Eden.

### Fortress Ruins

A walk through the cryptlike bowels of Slotsholmen, known as **Ruinerne under Christiansborg** (Map p40, C2; www.ses.dk; adult/child Dkr40/20; ☺10am-5pm daily, closed Mon Oct-Apr, guided tours in English noon Sat, in Danish noon Sun), offers a unique perspective on Copenhagen's well-seasoned history. In the basement of the current palace, beneath the tower, are the remains of two earlier castles. The most notable are the ruins of Absalon's fortress, Slotsholmen's original castle, built by Bishop Absalon in 1167.

### The Tower

A newer addition to the list of Christiansborg Slot attractions is the palace **tower** (tårnet; Map p40, C2; ☺11am-9pm Tue-Sun), which opened to the public for the first time in 2014. At 179m, it's the city's tallest tower, delivering a sweeping view of the Danish capital. The tower is also home to **Restaurant Tårnet** (www.taarnet.dk/restauranten; lunch

## ☑ Top Tip

▶ If you plan on visiting several of the sights at Christiansborg Slot, opt for the combination ticket. Costing Dkr110 (Dkr55 for children aged four to 17), it includes access to the Royal Reception Rooms, the Fortress Ruins and the Royal Stables. The ticket is valid for one month.

## ✕ Take a Break

During the warmer months, kick back with a coffee in the beautiful Royal Library Garden, which sits between Christiansborg Slot and the Dansk Jødisk Museum. While Christiansborg Slot's tower is home to the popular Restaurant Tårnet (p37), consider opting for the highly commended Søren K (p43), right on the waterfront inside the Royal Library.

smørrebrød Dkr85-135, dinner mains Dkr235; ⏱11.30am-3pm & 6-9.30pm Tue-Sun), owned by prolific restaurateur Rasmus Bo Bojesen. Lunch features contemporary smørrebrød (open sandwiches) and Danish cheeses; a better bet than the dinner, both in terms of value and the view. It's a popular nosh spot, so book ahead if you plan on staking out a table.

### Christiansborg Slotskirke

Tragedy struck CF Hansen's 19th-century neoclassical **Christiansborg Slotskirke** (Map p40, B1; ⏱10am-5pm Sun, daily Jul) on the day of the Copenhagen Carnival, 1992. A stray firework hit the scaffolding that had surrounded the church during a lengthy restoration and set the roof ablaze, destroying the dome. Miraculously, a remarkable frieze by Bertel Thorvaldsen that rings the ceiling just below the dome survived. The restorers went back to work and the church reopened in 1997.

### Royal Stables

Gallop your way through a collection of antique coaches, uniforms and riding paraphernalia at **De Kongelige Stalde** (Map p40, B3; Royal Stables; ☎33 40 10 10; www.kongehuset.dk; adult/child Dkr40/20; ⏱10am-5pm daily Jul, 1.30-4pm daily May, Jun & Sep, closed Mon Oct-Apr, guided tours in English 2pm Sat, in Danish 2pm Sun), some of which are still used for royal receptions. One of the highlights here is the Gold State Coach, traditionally used to transport the royal couple from Amalienborg Slot to the customary New Year's reception at Christiansborg Slot.

### Theatre Museum

Dating from 1767, the wonderfully atmospheric Hofteater (Old Court Theatre) has hosted everything from Italian opera to local ballet troupes, one of which included fledgling ballet student Hans Christian Andersen. Taking its current appearance in 1842, the venue is now the **Teatermuseet** (Map p40, B3; Theatre Museum; ☎33 11 51 76; www.teatermuseet.dk; Christiansborg Ridebane 18; adult/child Dkr40/free; ⏱11am-3pm Tue-Thu, 1-4pm Sat & Sun), and visitors are free to explore the stage, boxes and dressing rooms, along with displays of set models, drawings, costumes and period posters tracing the history of Danish theatre.

### Parliament Guided Tour

The 179 members of the Danish parliament debate national legislation in the **Folketinget** (Map p40, C3; ☎33 37 32 21; www.thedanishparliament.dk; Rigsdagsgården; admission free; ⏱guided tours in English 1pm Sun-Fri Jul–mid-Aug, reduced hours rest of year), accessible to visitors on a free guided tour. The tour also takes in Wanderer's Hall, which contains the original copy of the Constitution of the Kingdom of Denmark, enacted in 1849. Outside the summer high season, tours generally take place at 1pm on Sundays and public holidays – dates are listed on the website, where you can also book tour tickets.

Understand

## Christiansborg Slot's History

Christiansborg Slot is an architectural phoenix. The current palace is simply the latest in a series of buildings to have graced the site, among them medieval castles and an elegant baroque beauty.

### Bishop Absalon's Castle

According to medieval chronicler Saxo Grammaticus, Bishop Absalon of Roskilde built a castle on a small islet in the waters off the small town of Havn. The islet would become Slotsholmen, and the humble town Copenhagen. Erected in 1167 the castle was encircled by a limestone curtain wall, the ruins of which can still be seen today under the current complex. Despite frequent attacks, Absalon's creation stood strong for two centuries until a conflict between Valdemar IV of Denmark and the Hanseatic League saw the latter tear it down in 1369.

### Copenhagen Castle

By the end of the 14th century, the site was once again thriving, this time as the address of Copenhagen Castle. While the castle also featured a curtain wall, the new, improved model also came with a moat, as well as a solid, towered entrance. The castle remained the property of the Bishop of Roskilde until 1417, when Erik of Pomerania seized control, turning the castle into a royal abode. Nipped and tucked over time – Christian IV added a spire to the entrance tower – the castle was completely rebuilt by Frederik IV, evidently with dubious engineering advice. The castle began to crack under its own weight, leading to its hasty demolition in the 1730s.

### Christiansborg: One, Two, Three

The demolition led to the debut of the first Christiansborg Slot in 1745. Commissioned by Christian VI and designed by architect Elias David Häusser, it went up in flames in 1794, its only surviving remnant being the Royal Riding Complex, home to the Royal Stables. Rebuilt in the early 19th century, it became the seat of parliament in 1849 before once more succumbing to fire in 1884. In 1907 the cornerstone for the third Christiansborg Slot was laid by Frederik VIII. Designed by Thorvald Jørgensen and completed in 1928, it's a truly national affair, its neobaroque facade adorned with granite sourced from across the country.

Niels Juels Gade

Holmens Kanal

Nationalbanken

Havnegade

Christian IV's Bro

Knippelsbro

CHRISTIANSHAVN

Havnegade

Børsgade

Børsen ◉ 6

Slotsholmsgade

Christians Brygge

Holmens Kirke ◉ 7

Nikolaigade

Slotsholmens Kanal

Admiralgade

Boldhusgade

Laksegade

Ved Stranden

Holmens Bro

Ministerialbygning

Søren Kierkegaards Plads ◉ 8

Det Kongelige Bibliotek ◉ 2

◉ 9

Christiansborg Slotsplads

Vindebrogade

Højbro

Tøjhusgade

Det Kongelige Biblioteks Have

Dansk Jødisk Museum ◉ 4

◉ Christiansborg Slot

SLOTSHOLMEN

1 Thorvaldsens Museum ◉

Bertel Thorvaldsens Plads

Tøjhusmuseet

◉ 5

Christian IV's Bryghus

Kongernes Lapidarium ◉ 3

100 m
0.05 miles

Slotsholmens Kanal

Porthusgade

Snaregade

Magstræde

Knabrostræde

Nybrogade

Christiansborg Ridebane

Stormbro

Prinsensbro

Frederiksholms Kanal

Marmorbroen

Nationalmuseet

Ny Vestergade

Frederiksholms Kanal

Ny Kongensgade

Vester Voldgade

JORG GREUEL/GETTY IMAGES ©

Børsen (p43)

# Sights

### Thorvaldsens Museum    MUSEUM

1 ⊙ Map p40, B1

What looks like a colourful Graeco-Roman mausoleum is in fact a museum dedicated to the works of illustrious Danish sculptor Bertel Thorvaldsen (1770–1844). Heavily influenced by mythology after four decades in Rome, Thorvaldsen returned to Copenhagen and donated his private collection to the Danish public. In return the royal family provided this site for the construction of what is a remarkable complex housing Thorvaldsen's drawings, plaster moulds and statues. The museum also contains Thorvaldsens' own collection of Mediterranean antiquities. (www.thorvaldsensmuseum.dk; Bertel Thorvaldsens Plads; adult/child Dkr40/free, Wed free; ⏱10am-5pm Tue-Sun; 🚌1A, 2A, 11A, 26, 40, 66)

### Det Kongelige Bibliotek    LIBRARY

2 ⊙ Map p40, C4

Scandinavia's largest library consists of two very distinct parts: the original, 19th-century red-brick building and the head-turning 'Black Diamond' extension, the latter a leaning parallelogram of sleek black granite and smoke-coloured glass. From the soaring, harbour-fronting atrium, an escalator leads up to a 210-sq-metre

## Local Life
### Music at One

If you're inside Det Kongelige Bibliotek (p41) at 1pm, you'll be stopped in your tracks by *Katalog*, a specially commissioned sound installation by Danish composer Fuzzy. The three-minute electroacoustic work changes weekly, with one piece written for every week of the year. Each of the 52 dramatic compositions is inspired by one of the Royal Library's manuscripts, books, compositions or photographs.

ceiling mural by celebrated Danish artist Per Kirkeby. Beyond it, at the end of the corridor, is the 'old library' and its Hogwarts-like northern Reading Room, resplendent with vintage desk lamps and classical columns. (Royal Library; ☑ 33 47 47 47; www.kb.dk; Søren Kierkegaards Plads; admission free; ☺ 8am-7pm Mon-Sat Jul & Aug, to 10pm rest of year; ☐ 1A, 2A, 9A, 11A, 26, 40, 66, ☻ Det Kongelige Bibliotek)

## Kongernes Lapidarium   MUSEUM
3  ◉ Map p40, B4

Housed in Christian IV's old brewery, an extraordinary building dating from 1608, the Lapidarium of the Kings features original royal sculptures from Denmark's castles and gardens. Among these are the original 18th-century sandstone figures from Normandsdalen at Fredensborg Slot, unique in their depiction of common Norwegians and Faroese. Even more extraordinary is French sculptor JFJ Saly's 18th-century equestrian statue of Frederik V, more than 20 years in the making and more expensive than the entire Amalienborg Slot when completed. (Lapidarium of the Kings; www.kongerneslapidarium.dk; Frederiksholms Kanal 29; adult/child 4-17yr Dkr50/25; ☺ 10am-5pm daily May-Sep, closed Mon rest of year; ☐ 1A, 2A, 9A, 11A, 26, 40, 66, ☻ Det Kongelige Bibliotek)

## Dansk Jødisk Museum   MUSEUM
4  ◉ Map p40, C3

Designed by Polish-born Daniel Libeskind, the Danish Jewish Museum occupies the former Royal Boat House, an early 17th-century building once part of Christian IV's harbour complex. The transformed interior is an intriguing geometrical space, home to a permanent exhibition documenting Danish Jewry. You'll find the entrance on the Kongelige Bibliotekshave (Royal Library Garden), behind the Kongelige Bibliotek (Royal Library). (☑ 33 11 22 18; www.jewmus.dk; adult/child Dkr50/free; ☺ 10am-5pm Tue-Sun Jun-Aug, 1-4pm Tue-Fri, noon-5pm Sat & Sun rest of year; ☐ 1A, 2A, 11, 40, 66, 350S)

## Tøjhusmuseet   MUSEUM
5  ◉ Map p40, B3

The Royal Arsenal Museum houses a stunning collection of historic weaponry, from canons and medieval armour to pistols, swords and even a WWII flying bomb. Built by Christian IV in 1600, the 163m-long building is Europe's longest vaulted Renaissance hall. (Royal Danish Arsenal Museum; ☑ 33 11

60 37; natmus.dk/toejhusmuseet; Tøjhusgade 3; admission free; ⏰ noon-4pm Tue-Sun; 🚇 1A, 2A, 9A, 11A, 26, 40, 66)

## Børsen    HISTORIC BUILDING

6 ◉ Map p40, D2

Not many stock exchanges are topped by a 56m-tall spire formed from the entwined tails of four dragons. Børsen is one. Constructed at the eastern corner of Slotsholmen in the early 17th century, its elegant Dutch Renaissance design features richly embellished gables and an eye-catching copper roof. Opened during the bustling reign of Christian IV, this still-functioning chamber of commerce is the oldest in Europe, though generally not open to the public. (Børsgade; 🚇 1A, 2A, 9A, 40, 350S)

## Holmens Kirke    CHURCH

7 ◉ Map p40, D2

Queen Margrethe II took her marriage vows here in 1967, and while much of the present Dutch Renaissance–style structure dates from 1641, the church's nave was originally built in 1562 to be used as an anchor forge. Converted into a church for the Royal Navy in 1619, the building's burial chapel contains the remains of Admiral Niels Juel, who beat back the Swedes in the crucial 1677 Battle of Køge Bay. Other highlights include an intricately carved 17th-century oak altarpiece and pulpit. (Church of the Royal Danish Navy; www.holmenskirke.dk; Holmens Kanal 9; ⏰ 10am-4pm Mon, Wed, Fri & Sat, to 3.30pm Tue & Thu, noon-4pm Sun; 🚇 1A, 2A, 11, 29, 350S)

# Eating

## Søren K    MODERN DANISH $$

8 ✗ Map p40, D4

Bathed in light on even the dourest of days, the Royal Library's sleek, waterside fine-diner revels in showing off top-notch regional ingredients. Seasonal menus deliver delicate, contemporary takes on Nordic flavours, from smoked herring with gel of cress, egg yolk and radish to Norwegian lobster with cucumber, apple and sesame to buckwheat ice cream with buttermilk and woodruff. (📞 33 47 49 49; Søren Kierkegaards Plads 1; lunch dishes Dkr85-175, dinner mains Dkr190; ⏰ noon-4pm & 6-10pm Mon-Sat; 📶; 🚇 9A, 🚢 Det Kongelige Bibliotek)

## Øieblikket    CAFE $

9 ✗ Map p40, C4

The Royal Library's ground-floor cafe delivers a short menu of cheap, fresh bites, with one soup, a couple of salads and sandwiches, and no shortage of naughty cakes and pastries for a mid-afternoon high. The coffee is good and the harbourside deckchairs are a top spot to soak up some rays on those sunny summer afternoons. (Søren Kierkegaards Plads 1; soup & salads Dkr40-45, sandwiches Dkr50-55; ⏰ 8am-7pm Mon-Fri, 9am-6pm Sat; 📶✍; 🚇 9A, 🚢 Det Kongelige Bibliotek)

Explore

# Strøget & Around

Pedestrianised Strøget (pronounced 'stroll') weaves through Copenhagen's historical core from Rådhuspladsen to Kongens Nytorv. Technically consisting of five streets, it's a restless ribbon of shoppers and street performers of varying talent. The real gems are off the main drag: Strædet, the Latin Quarter, and the area bordered by Strøget, Købmagergade, Kronprinsensgade and Gothersgade.

# The Sights in a Day

☀️ Begin your saunter in the **Latin Quarter** (p48), taking in Bertel Thorvaldsen's acclaimed sculptures inside **Vor Frue Kirke** (p48) and exploring the jumble of bookshops, cafes, boutiques and centuries-old architecture on streets like Studiestræde, Krystalgade, Fiolstræde and Kannikestræde. At the eastern end of Kannikestræde stands **Rundetårn** (p48), worth climbing for the sweeping views.

☀️ Combine history and smørrebrød (open sandwiches) at local institution **Schønnemann** (p50). Alternatively, dig into contemporary Stone Age food at trendy **Palæo** (p51). The streets around Palæo are packed with inspired shops, including homegrown standouts **Han Kjøbenhavn** (p55), **Wood Wood** (p56), and **Hay House** (p55). Alternatively, opt for an afternoon of contemporary art at **Kunstforeningen GL Strand** (p49) and **Nikolaj Kunsthal** (p49).

🌙 Welcome the evening with a well-picked vino at **Ved Stranden 10** (p52) or gorgeous cocktails at **1105** (p52) or **Ruby** (p52), then chow at fun **Cock's & Cows** (p51) or oh-so-Frenchy **Brasserie Granberg** (p50). Cap the evening with a little night music at **Jazzhouse** (p54) or **La Fontaine** (p54), or indulge in a little wicked weekend clubbing at **Sunday** (p53).

 **Best of Copenhagen**

**Eating**
Schønnemann (p50)

Brasserie Granberg (p50)

**Drinking**
Ved Stranden 10 (p52)

1105 (p52)

Ruby (p52)

**Shopping**
Hay House (p55)

Illums Bolighus (p55)

Bruuns Bazaar (p55)

Stilleben (p55)

Han Kjøbenhavn (p55)

Storm (p56)

## Getting There

🚌 **Bus** Much of the compact city centre is pedestrianised, with major bus routes skirting the area. The only route that traverses the city core is route 11A; its stops include Kongens Nytorv and Nørreport stations, Vor Frue Kirke, and Gammeltorv (at Strøget). The bus also runs to Central Station and Nyhavn.

Ⓜ **Metro** Kongens Nytorv station is located just off the eastern end of Strøget. At the northwest edge of the city centre lies Nørreport station, which serves both the metro and S-train.

A
B
C
D

1

Ⓜ Nørreport

Nørreport
Ⓢ

11

Nansensgade

Nørre Farimagsgade

Rømersgade

Vendersgade

Israels
Plads

Linnesgade

Frederiksborggade

Rosenborggade

Hausergade

Kultorvet

Nørre Voldgade

Nørre Voldgade

Rosengården

Hvitfeldts Stræde

Peder
Hvitfeldts Stræde

2

Ørsteds
Parken

Nørregade

Fiolstræde

1 ◎
Latin
Quarter

Ⓐ 31

Krystalgade

**For reviews see**

| ◎ Sights | p48 |
| ✖ Eating | p50 |
| 🍷 Drinking | p52 |
| ★ Entertainment | p54 |
| 🔒 Shopping | p55 |

Teglgårdsstræde

Larslejsstræde

Københavns
Universitet

Kannikestræde

Vor Frue Plads

◎ 2

Klosterstræde

3

Sankt Pedersstræde

Larsbjørnsstræde

Studiestræde

18
Ⓧ

Vor Frue Kirke

Skindergade

Skoubogade

9 ✖

Gammeltorv

Nygade

Hammerichsgade

Studiestræde

Vester Voldgade

Vestergade

Nytorv

Brolæggerstræde

Knabrostræde

4

H C Andersens Blvd

Frederiksberggade

Kattesundet

Slutterigade

Kompagnistræde

22
★

Rådhusstræde

Lavendelstræde

Heste Gnægade

Farvergade

Jernbanegade

Rådhuspladsen

Regnbuepladsen

Løngangstræde

5

Axeltorv

**Vesterbrogade**

Tivoli

Rådhus
(City Hall)

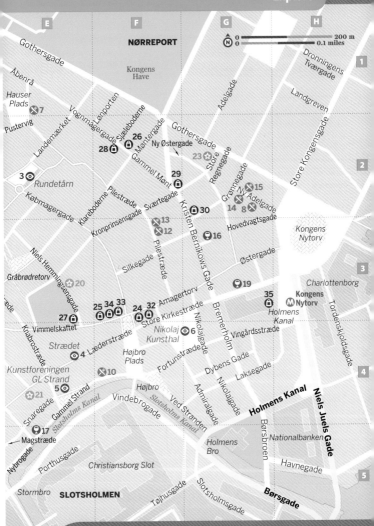

**NØRREPORT**

Gothersgade

Åbenrå

Hauser
Plads ✕7

Pustervig

Landemærket

Vognmagergade

Kongens
Have

Dronningens
Tværgade

Landgreven

Lønporten

Sjæleboderne

Møntergade

Adelgade

Gothersgade

Store Kongensgade

26

28 🔒

Gammel Mønt

Ny Østergade

23 ✪

Store Regnegade

3 ◉

Rundetårn

29

Grønnegade

Ny Adelgade

N✕15

Købmagergade

Klareboderne

Pilestræde

Kronprinsensgade

Svæartegade

30

14

8🔒

Niels Hemmingsensgade

Kristen Berníkows Gade

Hovedvagtsgade

Kongens
Nytorv

13

12

16

Gråbrødretorv

🔒20

Silkegade

Pilestræde

19

Østergade

Charlottenborg

27 🔒

Vimmelskaftet

25 34 33
🔒 🔒 🔒

24 32
🔒 🔒

Amagertorv

Store Kirkestræde

35
🔒

Ⓜ Kongens
Nytorv

Holmens
Kanal

Strædet

✕4 Læderstræde

Nikolaj
Kunsthal

Nikolaj ◉6

Bremerholm

Vingårdsstræde

Tordenskjoldsgade

Kunstforeningen
GL Strand

Højbro
Plads

Nikolajgade

Fortunstræde

Dybens Gade

Laksegade

5 🔒

✕10

Højbro

Ved Stranden

Admiralgade

Nikolajgade

Holmens Kanal

21

Snaregade

Gammel Strand

Slotsholms Kanal

Vindebrogade

Holmens
Bro

Niels Juels Gade

17

Magstræde

Slotsholms Kanal

Børsbroen

Nationalbanken

Nybrogade

Porthusgade

Christiansborg Slot

Holmens
Bro

Havnegade

Stormbro

**SLOTSHOLMEN**

Tøjhusgade

Slotsholmsgade

**Børsgade**

◎ N
0 ————— 200 m
0 ————— 0.1 miles

# Sights

### Latin Quarter
NEIGHBOURHOOD

1 ◎ Map p46, D2

Stretching east from Vor Frue Plads along Store Kannikestræde and Skindergade to Købmagergade, and north up Fiolstræde to Nørre Voldgade, the Latin Quarter gets its nickname from the presence of the old campus of Københavns Universitet (Copenhagen University) and the secondhand bookshops and cafes that grew up around it. It's a wonderful place for ambling, with postcard-pretty nooks including **Gråbrødretorv** (Grey Friars' Square),

## ☑ Top Tip

### Smart Bikes

Known as **Bycyklen** (City Bikes; bycyklen.dk), Copenhagen's state-of-the-art city bikes feature touchscreen GPS, multispeed electric motors, puncture-resistant tyres and locks. The bikes can be rented from a handful of docking stations dotted across the city, including Rådhuspladsen (City Hall Square) and Regnbuepladsen, as well as Central Station, Vesterport, Østerport and Dybbølsbro S-train stations. Accessible 24/7, 365 days a year, rental costs Dkr25 per hour and must be paid by credit card via the bike's touchscreen. For further information and a full list of docking stations, visit the Bycyklen website.

dating from the mid-17th century. (🚇11A, 5A, 6A, 14, Ⓜ Nørreport)

### Vor Frue Kirke
CHURCH

2 ◎ Map p46, D3

Founded in 1191 and rebuilt three times after devastating fires, Copenhagen's current cathedral dates from 1829, its neoclassical looks the work of CF Hansen. Sporting high-vaulted ceilings and columns, it's home to sculptor Bertel Thorvaldsen's statues of Christ and the apostles, completed in 1839 and considered his most acclaimed works. The sculptor's depiction of Christ, with comforting open arms, remains the most popular worldwide model for statues of Jesus. In May 2004, the cathedral hosted the wedding of Crown Prince Frederik to Australian Mary Donaldson. (www.koebenhavnsdomkirke. dk; Nørregade 8; ⊙8am-5pm, closed during services & concerts; 🚇11A)

### Rundetårn
HISTORIC BUILDING

3 ◎ Map p46, E2

Haul yourself to the top of the 34.8m-high red-brick 'Round Tower' and you will be following in the footsteps of such luminaries as King Christian IV, who built it in 1642 as an observatory for the famous astronomer Tycho Brahe. You'll also be following in the hoofsteps of Tsar Peter the Great's horse and, according to legend, the track marks of a car that made its way up the tower's spiral ramp in 1902. (Round Tower; www.rundetaarn. dk; Købmagergade 52; adult/child Dkr25/5; ⊙10am-8pm late May–late Sep, reduced hours

Vor Frue Kirke

rest of year, observatory usually 7-9pm Tue & Wed Oct & Mar, 6-9pm Tue & Wed Nov-Feb; 🚌5A, 14, 11A, Ⓜ Nørreport)

## Strædet    STREET

4 ◉ Map p46, E4

Parallel to crowded Strøget, Strædet is one of Copenhagen's eye-candy shopping streets. It's technically made up of two streets, Kompagnistræde and Læderstræde, with independent jewellers and antique silver shops. (🚌11A)

## Kunstforeningen GL Strand    GALLERY

5 ◉ Map p46, E4

The HQ of Denmark's artists' union continues to foster emerging and forward-thinking talent with five to six major exhibitions of modern and contemporary art each year. The work of both Danish and international artists is explored, with an underlying emphasis on current and emerging trends in the art world. (📞33 36 02 60; www.glstrand.dk; Gammel Strand 48; adult/child Dkr65/free; ⏰11am-5pm Tue & Thu-Sun, to 8pm Wed; 🚌1A, 2A, 11A, 26, 40, 66)

## Nikolaj Kunsthal    GALLERY

6 ◉ Map p46, G4

Constructed in the 13th century, the church of Skt. Nikolaj is now home to the Copenhagen Contemporary Art Centre, which hosts around half a dozen exhibitions every year.

**Local Life**

## Pisserenden

The cosy grid of shopping streets immediately to the north of Strøget, including Studiestræde, Larsbjørnsstræde and Vestergade, form **Pisserenden** (Map p46, B4; 🚌 26, 29, 33). A century or so ago this was a rather unsavoury part of town, full of brothels and bodegas (pubs). Pisserenden itself means 'The Pissoir' (a public urinal). These days, the quarter is a rather more pleasing blend of bohemian cafes, bars and vintage shops.

Exhibitions tend to focus on modern-day cultural, political and social issues, explored in mediums that are as diverse as photography and performance art. The centre also houses a snug and very well-regarded Danish restaurant called Maven. ( 🕿 33 18 17 80; www.nikolajkunsthal.dk; Nikolaj Plads 10; adult/child Dkr20/free, Wed free; 🕑 noon-5pm Tue, Wed & Fri-Sun, to 9pm Thu; 🚌 1A, 2A, 15, 19, 26, 350S, Ⓜ Kongens Nytorv)

## Eating

### Schønnemann                    DANISH $$

7 🍴 Map p46, E1

A verified institution, Schønnemann has been lining bellies with smørrebrød (open sandwiches) and snaps since 1877. Originally a hit with farmers in town peddling their produce, the restaurant's current fan base includes revered chefs like Noma's René Redzepi. Two smørrebrød per person should suffice, with standouts including the King's Garden (potatoes with smoked mayonnaise, fried onions, chives and tomato). Make sure to order both a beer and a glass of *snaps* to wash down the goodness, and always book ahead (or head in early) to avoid long lunchtime waits. ( 🕿 33 12 07 85; www.restaurantschonnemann.dk; Hauser Plads 16; smørrebrød Dkr72-178; 🕑 11.30am-5pm Mon-Sat; 🚌 6A, 11A, Ⓜ Nørreport)

### Brasserie Granberg          FRENCH $$

8 🍴 Map p46, G2

A whirl of chandeliers, vintage posters and crisp white linen, Gallic Granberg is the kind of place you expect to bump into a warbling Edith Piaf. Sink into an armchair, order a perfect G&T and browse a short, sharp menu of old faithfuls like lobster bisque with cognac, delicate *moules-frites* (mussels and fries) and obscenely fresh oysters. If it's winter, request a table in the super-snug back room. ( 🕿 33 12 45 32; www.brasseriegranberg.dk; Ny Adelgade 3; mains Dkr125-240; 🕑 5-10pm Tue-Fri & Sun, noon-10pm Sat; 🛜; 🚌 11A, Ⓜ Kongens Nytorv)

### La Glace                        BAKERY $

9 🍴 Map p46, D4

Copenhagen's oldest *konditori* (pastry shop) has been compromising waistlines since 1870. Succumb to a slice of the classic *valnøddekage* (walnut cake), a sinful concoction of crushed and caramelised walnuts, whipped cream and mocha glacé. Alternatively, betray your personal trainer with the *sportskage* (crushed nougat, cream and caramelised profiteroles). Your secret is safe. (www.laglace.dk; Skoubougade 3; cake slices Dkr57, pastries from Dkr36; ⊘8.30am-6pm Mon-Fri, 9am-6pm Sat, 10am-6pm Sun, closed Sun Easter-Sep; 🚊11A)

## Cock's & Cows
BURGERS $

10 🍴 Map p46, F4

When burger lust hits, satiate your urges at Cock's. In a setting best described as American diner meets Danish modernist, energetic staff deliver fresh, made-from-scratch burgers that are generous and insanely good. The meat is Danish and charcoal grilled, and there's a veggie burger for herbivores. Make sure to order a side of the onion rings. (📞69 69 60 00; www.cocksandcows.dk; Gammel Strand 34; burgers Dkr89-129; ⊘noon-9.30pm Sun-Thu, to 10.30pm Fri & Sat; 🚊1A, 2A, 26, 40, 66)

## Brdr.Price
INTERNATIONAL $$

11 🍴 Map p46, D1

Siblings Adam and James Price host a cult-status TV cooking show (Adam also created TV series *Borgen*), and their noshery turns prime produce into mood-enhancing comfort grub. Join foodies, *Borgen* fans and the odd poet in the bistro-style cafe for standouts like pillow-soft pulled pork served burger-style. Downstairs in the restaurant, chintzy chandeliers make a suitable match for old-school fare like lobster thermidor. (📞38 41 10 20;

http//:rosenborggade.brdr-price.dk; Rosenborggade 15-17; cafe mains Dkr145-195, restaurant mains Dkr175-265; ⊘cafe noon-midnight Sun-Thu, to 1am Fri & Sat, restaurant 5.30-10pm Sun-Wed, to 10.30pm Thu-Sat; 📶; 🚊6A, 11A, 150S, Ⓜ Nørrebro)

## Palæo
INTERNATIONAL $

12 🍴 Map p46, F3

Fast-food *Flintstones*-style is what you get at Palæo, a trendy eat-in/takeaway joint peddling so-called 'primal gastronomy'. Dishes are inspired by the palaeolithic diet, which means carb-light creations like hot dogs with egg-based wrappers (not buns) and risottos that give rice the flick for celeriac kernels. But if you're thinking mung bean mediocrity, think again: behind the menu is Michelin-starred chef Thomas Rode Andersen. (www.palaeo.dk; Pilestræde 32; dishes Dkr59-89; ⊘8am-8pm Mon-Fri, 10am-7pm Sat, 11am-5pm Sun; 📶; 🚊11A, Ⓜ Kongens Nytorv)

## 42° Raw
VEGETARIAN $$

13 🍴 Map p46, F3

Treat your body at this hip, healthy eat-in or takeaway. The deal is raw food served in vibrant, textured dishes like 'raw' lasagne, Thai noodles and sexed-up salads where strawberries mix it with watermelon and chilli. The handful of breakfast options include yoghurt and porridge, best washed down with organic coffee or a freshly squeezed juice or smoothies. Your mama will thanks us. (📞32 12 32 10; www.42raw.com; Pilestræde 32; meals Dkr88-128; ⊘7am-8pm

Mon-Fri, 10am-6pm Sat, 11am-5pm Sun; ⚲; 🚌11A)

## The Yogurt Shop YOGHURT $

14 🍴 Map p46, G2

Hay-designed chairs, flickering tea lights and piles of fashion mags – in Denmark, even yoghurt vendors make style editors weep. Join fashionistas and the virtuous as you decide just how to customise your yoghurt treat. Skyr, Greek or lactose-free yoghurt? Raspberry-ginger or strawberry-chilli purée? Granola topping or fresh fruit and nuts? First World problems never tasted so good. (www.theyogurtshop.dk; Ny Adelgade 7; yoghurt Dkr45-53; ⏰7.30am-6pm Mon-Fri, 10am-4pm Sat; 🛜; 🚌11A, Ⓜ Kongens Nytorv)

### Local Life
### Ved Stranden 10

Politicians and well-versed oeno-philes make a beeline for canalside wine bar **Ved Stranden 10** (Map p46, F4; www.vedstranden10.dk; Ved Stranden 10; ⏰noon-10pm Mon-Sat; 🛜; 🚌1A, 2A, 26, 40, 66), its vener-able cellar stocked with classic European vintages, biodynamic wines and obscure drops. Adorned with modernist Danish design and friendly, clued-in staff, its string of rooms lend the place an intimate, civilised air that's perfect for grown-up conversation. Chat ter-roir over vino-friendly nibbles like cheeses and smoked meats.

## Wokshop Cantina THAI $$

15 🍴 Map p46, G2

Communal tables and fresh Southeast Asian flavours are what you get at this popular basement cantina, a quick walk from Kongens Nytorv and the Hotel d'Angleterre. Tuck into staples like Thai fish cakes, *tom yam goong* soup, and no shortage of red, green and yellow curries. (www.wokshop.dk; Ny Adelgade 6; noodle dishes Dkr65-129, dinner mains Dkr129-169; ⏰noon-10pm Mon-Sat; 🚌11A, Ⓜ Kongens Nytorv)

# Drinking

## 1105 COCKTAIL BAR

16 🍷 Map p46, G3

Head in before 11pm for a bar seat at this dark, luxe cocktail lounge. It's the domain of world-renowned barman Hardeep Rehal, who made the top 10 at the 2014 Diageo World Class, the unofficial Olympics of mixology. While Rehal's martini is the stuff of legend, 1105's seductive libations include both classics and classics with a twist. Whisky con-noisseurs will be equally enthralled. (www.1105.dk; Kristen Bernikows Gade 4; ⏰8pm-2am Wed, Thu & Sat, 4pm-2am Fri; 🚌11A, Ⓜ Kongens Nytorv)

## Ruby COCKTAIL BAR

17 🍷 Map p46, E5

Cocktail connoisseurs raise their glasses to high-achieving Ruby. Here,

Cinemateket (p54)

hipster-geek mixologists whip up near-flawless libations such as the Green & White (vodka, dill, white chocolate and liquorice root) and a lively crowd spills into a labyrinth of cosy, decadent rooms. For a gentlemen's club vibe, head downstairs into a world of Chesterfields, oil paintings and wooden cabinets lined with spirits. (www.rby.dk; Nybrogade 10; ⊙4pm-2am Mon-Sat, 7pm-1am Sun; ⬚1A, 2A, 11A, 26, 40, 66)

## Jailhouse CPH
GAY

18 🔵 Map p46, C3

Trendy, attitude-free and particularly popular with an older male crowd, this themed bar promises plenty of penal action, with uniformed 'guards'

and willing guests. (www.jailhousecph.dk; Studiestræde 12; ⊙3pm-2am Sun-Thu, to 5am Fri & Sat; 🛜; ⬚5A, 6A, 11A)

## Sunday
CLUB

19 🔵 Map p46, G3

Club meisters Simon Frank and Simon Lennet are known for whipping up exclusive, cult-status clubs with kinky or subversive twists. Sunday is no exception, with Bangkok lady-boy servers and hedonistic party people with an anything-goes attitude. Lose your inhibitions over electro, rock, hip hop and RnB. (☎53 66 82 28; www.sundayclub.dk; Lille Kongensgade 16; ⊙11.30pm-5am Fri & Sat; Ⓜ Kongens Nytorv)

# Entertainment

### Jazzhouse

JAZZ

20 ⭐ Map p46, E3

Copenhagen's leading jazz joint serves up top Danish and visiting talent, with music styles running the gamut from bebop to fusion jazz. Doors usually open at 7pm, with concerts starting at 8pm. On Friday and Saturday, late-night concerts (from 11pm) are also offered. Check the website for details and consider booking big-name acts in advance. (☎ 33 15 47 00; www.jazzhouse.dk; Niels Hemmingsensgade 10; 🚇11A)

### La Fontaine

JAZZ

21 ⭐ Map p46, E4

Cosy and intimate, Copenhagen's jazz club veteran is a great spot to catch emerging home-grown musicians and the occasional big name. If you're an aspiring jazz star, hang around until late, when the stage is thrown open to songbirds in the audience. (www.lafontaine.dk; Kompagnistræde 11; ⏰8pm-5am daily, live music from 10pm Fri & Sat, from 9pm Sun; 🚇1A, 2A, 11A, 26, 40, 66)

### Huset KBH

LIVE MUSIC

22 ⭐ Map p46, D5

Huset KBH is an institution, churning out almost 1500 annual events spanning live music, theatre and arthouse film, to poetry slams, cabaret and stand-up comedy. The complex also houses a waste-free restaurant using surplus produce donated from the food industry, with all profits going towards humanitarian projects in Sierra Leone. (☎ 21 51 21 51; www. huset-kbh.dk; Rådhusstræde 13; ⏰hours vary, restaurant 6-9pm Tue-Sat; 🛜; 🚇1A, 2A, 11A, 26, 40, 66)

### Jazzhus Montmartre

JAZZ

23 ⭐ Map p46, G2

One of Scandinavia's great jazz venues, Jazzhus Montmartre showcases local and international talent. On concert nights, you can also tuck into Italian-inspired pre-show nosh (three-course set menu Dkr325, charcuterie plate Dkr165) at the cafe-restaurant, run by the team from Michelin-starred restaurant Era Ora. (☎ 70 26 32 67; www.jazzhusmontmartre.dk; Store Regnegade 19A; ⏰5.30-11.30pm Thu-Sat; 🚇11A, 350S, Ⓜ Kongens Nytorv)

---

◯ Local Life

#### Cinemateket

Local cinephiles flock to the Danish Film Institute's cinema centre, **Cinemateket** (Map p46, F1; www.dfi. dk; Gothersgade 55; ⏰9.30am-10pm Tue-Fri, noon-10pm Sat, noon-7.30pm Sun; 🚇11A, 350S). It screens over 60 films per month, including semimonthly classic Danish hits (with English subtitles) on Sundays. The centre also houses an extensive library of film and TV literature, and a 'videotheque' with more than 1500 titles.

# Shopping

## Hay House
DESIGN

**24** 🔒 Map p46, F3

Rolf Hay's fabulous interior design store sells its own coveted line of furniture, textiles and design objects, as well as those of other fresh, innovative Danish designers. Easy-to-pack gifts include anything from notebooks and ceramic cups to building blocks for style-savvy kids. There's a second branch at Pilestræde 29-31. (www.hay.dk; Østergade 61; ⏰10am-6pm Mon-Fri, to 5pm Sat; 🚌11A)

## Illums Bolighus
DESIGN

**25** 🔒 Map p46, F3

Revamp everything from your wardrobe to your living room at this multi-level department store, dedicated to big names in Danish and international design. Coveted goods include fashion, jewellery, silverware and glassware, and no shortage of Danish furniture, textiles and fetching office accessories. (www.illumsbolighus.dk; Amagertorv 8-10; ⏰10am-7pm Mon-Fri, to 6pm Sat, 11am-6pm Sun; 🚌11A)

## Bruuns Bazaar
FASHION

**26** 🔒 Map p46, F2

You'll find both men's and women's threads at the flagship store for Bruuns Bazaar, one of Denmark's most coveted and internationally respected brands. The style is contemporary, archetypal Scandinavian, with a focus on modern daywear that's crisp, well-cut and classically chic with a twist. (www.bruunsbazaar.com; Vognmagergade 2; ⏰10am-6pm Mon-Thu, to 7pm Fri, to 5pm Sat; 🚌11A, 350S)

## Stilleben
DESIGN

**27** 🔒 Map p46, E3

Owned by Danish Design School graduates Ditte Reckweg and Jelena Schou Nordentoft, Stilleben stocks a bewitching range of contemporary ceramic, glassware, jewellery and textiles from mostly emerging Danish and foreign designers. A must for design fans and savvy shoppers seeking 'Where did you get that?' gifts. (📞33 91 11 31; www.stilleben.dk; Niels Hemmingsensgade 3; ⏰10am-6pm Mon-Fri, to 5pm Sat; 🚌11A)

## Han Kjøbenhavn
FASHION, ACCESSORIES

**28** 🔒 Map p46, F2

While we love the modernist fit-out, it's what's on the racks that will hook you: original, beautifully crafted men's threads that merge Scandinavian sophistication with hints of old-school Danish working-class culture. Accessories include painfully cool eyewear, as well as sublime leathergoods from America's Kenton Sorensen. (www.hankjobenhavn.com; Vognmagergade 7; ⏰11am-6pm Mon-Thu, to 7pm Fri, 10am-5pm Sat; 🚌11A, Ⓜ Kongens Nytorv)

## Storm

FASHION, ACCESSORIES

**29** 🔒 Map p46, F2

Storm is one of Copenhagen's most inspired fashion pit stops, with trend-setting men's and women's labels such as Chauncey, Géométrick and Merz b. Schwanen. The vibe is youthful and street smart, with extras including statement sneakers, boutique fragrances, art and design tomes, fashion magazines and jewellery. Obligatory for cashed-up hipsters. (www.stormfashion.dk; Store Regnegade 1; ⏰11am-5.30pm Mon-Thu, to 7pm Fri, 10am-4pm Sat; 🚌11A, Ⓜ Kongens Nytorv)

## Wood Wood

FASHION, ACCESSORIES

**30** 🔒 Map p46, G2

Unisex Wood Wood's flagship store is a veritable who's who of cognoscenti street-chic labels. Top of the heap are Wood Wood's own hipster-chic creations, made with superlative fabrics and attention to detail. The supporting cast includes solid knits from classic Danish brand SNS Herning, wallets from Comme des Garçons and sunglasses from Kaibosh. (www.woodwood.dk;

☑ Top Tip

### To Shop or Not

Many of Copenhagen's museums are closed on Mondays (especially outside the summer season), making Monday the ideal day for a little Danish retail therapy. The worst day to shop is Sunday, when many stores are shut.

Grønnegade 1; ⏰10.30am-6pm Mon-Thu, to 7pm Fri, to 5pm Sat; 🚌11A, Ⓜ Kongens Nytorv)

## Henrik Vibskov

FASHION

**31** 🔒 Map p46, D2

Not just a drummer and prolific artist, Danish *enfant terrible* Henrik Vibskov pushes the fashion envelope too. Break free with his bold, bright, creatively silhouetted threads for progressive guys and girls, as well as other fashion-forward labels such as Issey Miyake, Walter Van Beirendonck and Denmark's own Stine Goya. (www. henrikvibskov.com; Krystalgade 6; ⏰11am-6pm Mon-Thu, to 7pm Fri, to 5pm Sat; 🚌11A, Ⓜ Nørreport, 🚉S-train Nørreport)

## Le Klint

HOMEWARES

**32** 🔒 Map p46, F3

Beautiful lighting is a Scandinavian obsession and Le Klint's handmade, concertina-style lampshades are works of art in themselves. Designed by some of Denmark's most respected designers and architects, the range includes ceiling, table and wall lamps, mostly in classic white. (📞33 11 66 63; www.leklint.com; Store Kirkestræde 1; ⏰10am-6pm Tue-Fri, to 4pm Sat; 🚌1A, 2A, 11A, 26, 40, 66, Ⓜ Kongens Nytorv)

## Georg Jensen

DESIGN

**33** 🔒 Map p46, F3

This is the world-famous silversmith's flagship store, selling everything from rings, brooches and watches to attention-commanding vases and

Georg Jensen on pedestrianised Strøget

tableware. Popular gifts for less than Dkr300 include moneyclips and business-card holders, as well as Georg Jensen's iconic elephant bottle opener. (☎33 11 40 80; www.georgjensen. com; Amagertorv 4; ◷10am-7pm Mon-Fri, to 6pm Sat, 11am-4pm Sun; 🚊11A)

### Royal Copenhagen Porcelain
PORCELAIN

**34** 🅐 Map p46, F3

This is the main showroom for the historic Royal Danish Porcelain, one of the city's best-loved souvenir choices. Its 'blue fluted' pattern is famous around the world, as is the painfully expensive Flora Danica dinner service, its botanical illustra-

tions the work of 18th-century painter, Johann Christoph Bayer. (☎33 13 71 81; www.royalcopenhagen.com; Amagertorv 6; ◷10am-7pm Mon-Fri, to 6pm Sat, 11am-4pm Sun; 🚊11A, Ⓜ Kongens Nytorv)

### Magasin
DEPARTMENT STORE

**35** 🅐 Map p46, G3

The city's largest (and oldest) department store covers an entire block of Kongens Nytorv. Beyond the global fashion brands are a handful of savvy local labels, including Mads Nørgaard, Henrik Vibskov and Baum und Pferdgarten. Head to the basement for international magazines. (☎33 11 44 33; www.magasin.dk; Kongens Nytorv 13; ◷10am-8pm; 🚊1A, 11A, 26, Ⓜ Kongens Nytorv)

Explore

# Nyhavn & the Royal Quarter

Flanked by colourful, Dutch-style town houses, photogenic canal Nyhavn (*noo-houn*) was built in the 17th century to link the harbour to the city. North of it lies the royal quarter, Frederiksstaden. It's here that you'll find the royal pad Amalienborg Slot, pompous Marmorkirken and Designmuseum Danmark. Frederiksstaden stretches north towards Kastellet fortress and *that* little mermaid.

## The Sights in a Day

☀ Fuel up with breakfast at **Union Kitchen** (p67), then head east along Nyhavn to the harbour. Turn left and you'll hit **Skuespilhuset** (p67), the city's striking contemporary playhouse. Continue north along the waterfront to royal residence **Amalienborg Slot** (p64). Drop in on the palace museum or continue to the flamboyantly rococo **Marmorkirken** (p64). From here, **Designmuseum Danmark** (p60) is a quick walk up Bredgade.

☀ After lunching at the museum, head north to old fortress **Kastellet** (p64) and explore its eccentric gaggle of historic buildings. If you simply insist on dropping in on the **Little Mermaid** (p66), you'll find it just to the east of Kastellet, right in the harbour. Close by is artist Bjørn Nørgaard's more dystopian modern version.

☾ Reserve a table at **Clou** (p65) or **Damindra** (p66) for a degustation dinner you won't forget, or dream of the Tuscan sun at organic **Ché Fè** (p66). Cheque signed, try your luck finding sneaky speakeasy **Union Bar** (p67) for sassy cocktails and a New York City vibe. For something extra romantic, reserve tickets to the ballet or the opera at **Det Kongelige Teater** (p67).

### ◉ Top Sights
Designmuseum Danmark (p60)

### 💜 Best of Copenhagen
**Museums & Galleries**
Designmuseum Danmark (p60)

Kunsthal Charlottenborg (p64)

**Eating**
Clou (p65)

Damindra (p66)

**Drinking**
Union Bar (p67)

Forloren Espresso (p67)

### Getting There

Ⓜ **Metro** Kongens Nytorv station lies 200m southwest of Nyhavn.

🚌 **Bus** Route 1A runs north along Bredgade and back south along Store Kongensgade. Routes 11A and 66 cross the eastern end of Nyhavn, stopping at Skuespilhuset. Route 26 runs along the southern end of Bredgade, then along Dronningens Tværgade and Borgergade.

## Top Sights
# Designmuseum Danmark

Don't know your Egg from your Swan? What about your PH4 from your PH5? For a crash course in Denmark's incredible design heritage, make an elegant beeline for Designmuseum Danmark. Housed in a converted 18th-century hospital, the museum is a must for fans of the applied arts and industrial design, its booty including Danish silver and porcelain, textiles and the iconic design pieces of modern innovators like Kaare Klint, Poul Henningsen, Arne Jacobsen and Verner Panton.

◎ Map p18; C4

www.designmuseum.dk

Bredgade 68

adult/child Dkr75/free

🕙11am-5pm Tue & Thu-Sun, to 9pm Wed

🚍1A

Designer furniture, Designmuseum Danmark

# Don't Miss

### Utopia & Reality

*Utopia & Reality* is the museum's main permanent exhibition, exploring 20th-century industrial design and crafts in the context of social, economic, technological and theoretical changes. Displaying celebrated furniture and applied arts from both Denmark and abroad, the collection's more unusual highlights include the PH Grand Piano, conceived by legendary Danish lighting designer, Poul Henningsen. Another unexpected delight is the collection of vintage graphic posters, which includes the work of Viggo Vagnby, creator of the iconic 1959 'Wonderful Copenhagen' poster, depicting a duck and her little ones stopping city traffic.

### Fashion & Fabric

*Fashion & Fabric* is Designmuseum Danmark's newest permanent exhibition. Launched in December 2014, the space showcases around 350 objects from the museum's rich textile and fashion collections. Spanning four centuries, the collection's treasures include French and Italian silks, ikat and batik weaving, and two extraordinary mid-20th-century tapestries based on cartoons by Henri Matisse. As would you expect, Danish textiles and fashion feature prominently, including Danish *hedebo* embroidery from the 18th to 20th centuries, and Erik Mortensen's collection of haute couture frocks from French fashion houses Balmain and Jean-Louis Scherrer.

## ☑ Top Tip

▶ The museum shop is one of the city's best and a great place to pick up some savvy gifts. You'll find art, craft and design tomes; funky textiles, ceramics, glassware and jewellery; industrial design pieces; and easy-to-carry souvenirs sans the tack.

## ✗ Take a Break

Rehydrate or grab a bite at the museum's decent Klint Cafe, located just off the museum lobby. Food options focus on Danish classics and the outdoor courtyard is a fine spot to restore yourself in the warmer months.

Little Mermaid

Yderhavnen

Langelinie

ØSTERPORT

Ⓢ Østerport

Folke Bernadottes Allé

Oslo Plads

2 ◎ Kastellet

Smedelinien

Churchillparken

Esplanaden

Grønningen

Store Kongensgade

Larsens Plads

Yderhavnen

Designmuseum Danmark

Bredgade

Fredericiagade

Gernersgade

Skt Pauls Gade

Kronprinsessegade

Klerkegade

Borgergade

Rigensgade

Øster Voldgade

Østre Anlæg

Sølvgade

Kongens Have

CHRISTIANSHAVN

Holmen

Orlogsværftvej

Papirøen (Paper Island)

Inderhavnen

Kvæsthusgraven

200 m
0.1 miles

Toldbodgade

Amaliehaven

Amalienborg plads

Kvæsthusgade

Toldbodgade

🎯11

Amaliegade

Sankt Annæ Plads

Amalienborg Slot 🎯1

Marmorkirken Frederiksgade

Amaliegade

Nyhavn

Nyhavnsbro

Holbergsgade

NYHAVN

Bredgade

Strandstr.

Nyhavn

Nyhavn

✕9

Holbergsgade

🅿️6

Holbergsgade

Havnegade

Store Strandstr.

Heluf Trolles Gade

✕10

Helsingørsgade

Peder Skrams Gade

Dronningens Tværgade

✕7

13🏠

Kunsthal Charlottenborg

Tordenskjoldsgade

Landgreven

Store Kongensgade

🏠14

Kongens Nytorv

🎯12

Niels Juels Gade

Bredgade

✕8

✕5

Holmens Kanal

Adelgade

Gothersgade

Ny Adelgade

Hovedvagtsgade

Østergade

Lille Kongensgade

Holmens Kanal

Laksegade

Ny Østergade

Bremerholm

Højbro Plads

Fortunstræde

Dybens Gade

Holmens Bro

Kronprinsessegade

# Sights

## Amalienborg Slot

PALACE

1 ⦿ Map p62, C5

Home of the current queen, Margrethe II, Amalienborg Slot consists of four austere, 18th-century palaces around a large cobbled square. The changing of the guard takes place here daily at noon, the new guard having marched through the city centre from the barracks on Gothersgade at 11.30am. One of the palaces features exhibits of the royal apartments used by three generations of the monarchy from 1863 to 1947, its reconstructed rooms decorated with gilt-leather tapestries, *trompe-l'œil* paintings, family photographs and antiques. (☑ 33 12 21 86; www.dkks.dk; Amalienborg Plads; adult/child Dkr90/free; ⦿ 10am-4pm daily May-Oct, reduced hours rest of year; ⏹ 1A, 26)

---

☑ Top Tip

### Changing of the Guard

The changing of the guard takes place in the courtyard of Amalienborg Slot daily at noon. The new guard commence their march at 11.30am from the barracks on Gothersgade, right beside Kongens Have, marching down Rosenborggade, Købmagergade, Østergade, Kongens Nytorv, Bredgade, Snkt Annæ Plads and Amaliegade on their way.

---

## Kastellet

FORTRESS

2 ⦿ Map p62, D1

The star-shaped fortress of Kastellet was originally commissioned by Frederik III in 1662. Today it is one of the most historically evocative sites in the city, its grassy ramparts and moat surrounding some beautiful 18th-century barracks, as well as a chapel occasionally used for concerts. On the ramparts is a historic windmill and some excellent views to the Little Mermaid, the harbour and, in the other direction, Marmorkirken. (⏹ 1A, ⏹ Nordre Toldbod)

## Kunsthal Charlottenborg

MUSEUM

3 ⦿ Map p62, B7

Fronting Kongens Nytorv, Charlottenborg was built in 1683 as a palace for the royal family. Home to Det Kongelige Kunstakademi (Royal Academy of Fine Arts) since 1754, it keeps culture vultures flocking with its rotating exhibitions of contemporary art from both Danish and international artists. (☑ 33 74 46 39; www.kunsthalcharlottenborg.dk; Nyhavn 2; adult/child Dkr60/free, after 5pm Wed free; ⦿ 11am-5pm Tue & Thu-Sun, to 8pm Wed; ⏹ 1A, 15, 19, 26, 350S, Ⓜ Kongens Nytorv)

## Marmorkirken

CHURCH

4 ⦿ Map p62, C5

Consecrated in 1894, the neobaroque Marble Church (officially Frederikskirken) is one of Copenhagen's most

Kastellet

imposing architectural assets. Its grandiose dome – measuring more than 30m in diameter and inspired by St Peter's in Rome – can be climbed on weekends. The church was ordered by Frederik V and drawn up by Nicolai Eigtved. Construction began in 1749 but spiralling costs saw the project mothballed. Salvation came in the form of Denmark's wealthiest 19th-century financier CF Tietgen, who bankrolled the project's revival. (Marble Church; ☎33 15 01 44; www.marmorkirken. dk; Frederiksgade 4; church free, dome adult/child Dkr35/20; ⏰church 10am-5pm Mon, Tue, Thu & Sat, 10am-6.30pm Wed, noon-5pm Fri & Sun, dome 1pm & 3pm daily mid-Jun–Aug, 1pm & 3pm Sat & Sun rest of year; 🚌1A)

# Eating

## Clou                        MODERN DANISH $$$

5 🍴 Map p62, B5

Michelin-starred Clou luxuriates in its large, linen-clad tables, upholstered armchair, and bowtied waiters in armbands. That said, the menu is an adventurous, modern affair, with both Nordic and global influences driving knockouts like duck breast served with luscious berries and chestnuts braised in aniseed and maple syrup. As for the wines: they're so impressive that the food is created around them. (☎36 16 30 00; www. restaurant-clou.dk; Borgergade 16; 3/5/7-course menu incl wine Dkr850/1300/1600; ⏰6-9pm Tue-Sat; 🚌1A, 11A, 26, Ⓜ Kongens Nytorv)

## Damindra

JAPANESE $$$

6  Map p62, C7

We wouldn't be surprised if Japanese Damindra lands a Michelin star in the next few years. From the buttery sashimi to an unforgettable prawn tempura, dishes are obscenely fresh and mesmerising. The evening 'Chef's Choice' set sushi menu (Dkr398) provides the perfect culinary tour, while desserts such as green tea ice cream with plum compote and fresh wasabi cream make for a wicked epilogue. (☎33 12 33 75; www.damindra. dk; Holbergsgade 26; lunch dishes Dkr175-398, 7-course dinner tasting menu Dkr750; ⏱11am-3pm & 5-10pm Tue-Sat; ▣11A, 66, Ⓜ Kongens Nytorv)

## Meyers Bageri

BAKERY $

7  Map p62, B5

Sugar and spice and all things nice is what you get at this pocket-sized organic bakery, owned by the found-ing father of the New Nordic food movement, Claus Meyer. Only flour produced in-house is good enough for these sticky morsels, among them golden apple croissants, *blåbærsnur-rer* (blueberry twists) and a luscious *kanelsnegle* (cinnamon snail) laced with *remonce* (creamed butter and sugar filling). (www.clausmeyer.dk; Store Kongensgade 46; pastries from Dkr20; ⏱7am-6pm Mon-Fri, to 4pm Sat, to 1pm Sun; ▣1A, 26, Ⓜ Kongens Nytorv)

## Ché Fè

ITALIAN $$

8  Map p62, B5

With its rustic farmhouse chairs, swathes of hessian and colourful ceramics, Ché Fè feels freshly plucked out of a Tuscan hillside. Whatever the weather, expect warm, soulful Italian dishes like housemade pasta with venison, or earthy Tuscan pork sausage with tomato sauce and black chickpeas. The set menu (Dkr250) is good value, especially given that most

---

### Understand
#### The Little Mermaid

Love it or loathe it, when the world thinks of Copenhagen, the **Little Mermaid** (Den Lille Havfrue; Map p62, E1; ▣1A, ⛴Nordre Toldbod) often springs to mind. Alas, many people do seem to loathe this tiny statue of one of Hans Christian Andersen's most famous characters. Commissioned by Carlsberg Brewery and created by sculptor Edvard Eriksen in 1913, the fin-tipped local has been vandalised repeatedly, losing her head and arms more than once. In 2006 Carlsberg commissioned Bjørn Nørgaard (among others) to create a new Little Mermaid. The Danish artist came up with a 'genetically altered' version that sits not far from the original beside the harbour and is, in fact, probably truer in spirit to the rather bleak, twisted Andersen fairy tale.

of the ingredients are organic. Viva Ché Fè! (☎33 11 17 21; www.biotrattoria.dk; Borgergade 17A; mains Dkr150-195; ⏰6-10pm Mon-Sat; 🛜; 🚌11A, 26, Ⓜ Kongens Nytorv)

## Union Kitchen
CAFE $$

9 🍴 Map p62, C6

Just around the corner from Nyhavn is new-school Union Kitchen, where inked staffers look like punk-pop rockers, the colour scheme is grey-on-grey and the clipboard menu is packed with contemporary cafe grub like home-made granola and toasted sourdough with cottage cheese, tomato, thyme and olive oil. Best of all is the 'Balls of the Day', a daily-changing combo of succulent homemade meatballs served with interesting sides. (Store Strandstræde 21; ⏰7.30am-5pm Mon & Tue, to 11pm Wed & Thu, to midnight Fri, 8am-midnight Sat, 8am-5pm Sun; 🛜; 🚌11A, 66, Ⓜ Kongens Nytorv)

# Drinking

## Union Bar
BAR

10 🍷 Map p62, B6

Inspired by the speakeasy bars of old New York (even the cocktails are named after 1920s slang), the sneaky Union lies behind an unmarked black door. Ring the buzzer and head down the steps to a suitably dim, decadent scene of handsome bartenders, in-the-know revellers and silky tunes. (www.theunion-bar.dk; Store Strandstræde 16; ⏰8pm-2am Tue-Thu, 4pm-3am Fri, 8pm-3am Sat)

# Entertainment

## Skuespilhuset
THEATRE

11 ⭐ Map p62, D7

Copenhagen's handsome, contemporary playhouse is home to the Royal Danish Theatre and a world-class repertoire of home-grown and foreign plays. Productions range from the classics to provocative contemporary works. Tickets often sell out well in advance, so book ahead if you're set on a particular production. (☎33 69 69 69; www.kglteater.dk; Sankt Anne Plads 36; 🚌11A, Ⓜ Kongens Nytorv)

## Det Kongelige Teater
BALLET, OPERA

12 ⭐ Map p62, B7

These days, the main focus of the opulent Gamle Scene ('old stage') is world-class opera and ballet, including productions from the Royal Danish Ballet. The current building, the fourth theatre to occupy the site, was completed in 1872 and designed by Vilhelm

## Understand

# Danish Design

Visit a Copenhagen home and you'll invariably find Poul Henningsen lamps hanging from the ceiling, Arne Jacobsen or Hans Wegner chairs in the dining room, and the table set with Royal Copenhagen dinner sets, Georg Jensen cutlery and Bodum glassware. Here, good design is not just for museums and institutions: it's an integral part of daily life.

### Iconic Chairs

Modern Danish furniture is driven by the principle that design should be tailored to the comfort of the user – a principle most obvious in Denmark's world-famous designer chairs. Among the classics are Hans Wegner's Round Chair (1949). Proclaimed 'the world's most beautiful chair' by US *Interiors* magazine in 1950, it would find fame as the chair used by Nixon and Kennedy in their televised presidential debates in 1960. The creations of modernist architect Arne Jacobsen are no less iconic. Designed for Copenhagen's Radisson Blu Royal Hotel, the Egg Chair (1958) is the essence of jet-setting mid-century modernity. His revolutionary Ant Chair (1952), the model for stacking chairs found in schools and cafeterias worldwide, found infamy as the chair on which call girl Christine Keeler (from the British Profumo Affair) sits in a 1960s Lewis Morley photograph.

### Switched-On Lighting

Danish design prevails in stylish lamps as well. The country's best-known lamp designer was Poul Henningsen (1894–1967), who emphasised the need for lighting to be soft, for the shade to cast a pleasant shadow and for the light bulb to be blocked from direct view. His PH5 lamp (1958) remains one of the most popular hanging lamps sold in Denmark today. The popularity of fellow modernist designer Verner Panton is no less enduring. Like Henningsen, Panton was interested in creating lighting that hid the light source, a goal achieved to playful effect with his signature Flowerpot lamp (1968). The designer, who worked for Arne Jacobsen's architectural office from 1950 to 1952, would also go down as an innovative furniture designer, his plastic single-piece Panton Chair (1967) one of the 20th century's most famous furniture pieces.

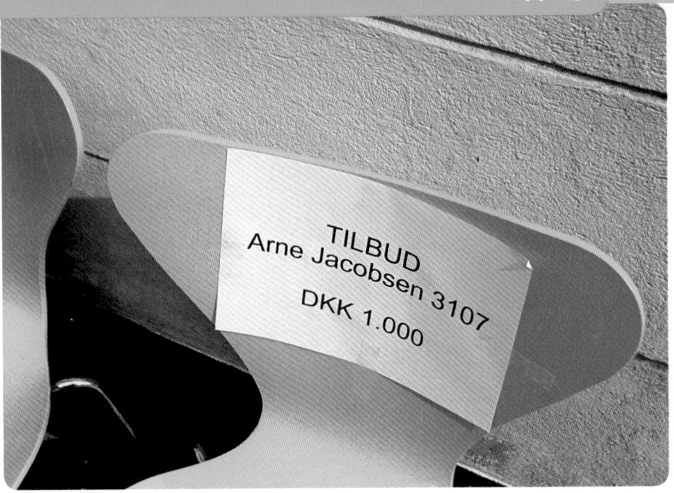




Arne Jacobsen chairs for sale

Dahlerup and Ove Petersen. Book tickets in advance. (Royal Theatre; ☎33 69 69 69; www.kglteater.dk; Kongens Nytorv; 🚌1A, 11A, 20E, 26, 350S, Ⓜ Kongens Nytorv)

## Shopping

### Klassik Moderne Møbelkunst — FURNITURE

13 🛍 Map p62, B6

Close to Kongens Nytorv, Klassik Moderne Møbelkunst is Valhalla for lovers of Danish design, with a trove of classics from greats like Poul Henningsen, Hans J Wegner, Arne Jacobsen, Finn Juhl and Nanna Ditzel – in other words, a veritable museum of Scandinavian furniture from the mid-20th century. (☎33 33 90 60; www.klassik.dk; Bredgade 3; ⏰11am-6pm Mon-Fri, 10am-3pm Sat; 🚌1A, 11A, 20E, 26, 350S, Ⓜ Kongens Nytorv)

### Susanne Juul — HATS

14 🛍 Map p62, B6

Crown Princess Mary is known to ride her bike here occasionally, which is hardly surprising given that Susanne Juul is considered one of Copenhagen's finest milliners. The look is classic and refined, from the felt hats and fascinators to the dapper caps and hats for men. Prices start at around Dkr375 and soar from there. (☎33 32 25 22; www.susannejuul.dk; Store Kongensgade 14; ⏰11am-5.30pm Tue-Thu, to 6pm Fri, 10am-2pm Sat; 🚌1A, 11A, 26, Ⓜ Kongens Nytorv)

Explore

# Christianshavn

Handsome canals, quirky churches and verdant city ramparts make Christianshavn (*Christians-houn*) one of Copenhagen's prettiest quarters. The island is mostly residential, home to not-really-struggling artists, yuppies doing their best to look relaxed and bohemian, and a large Greenlandic community. In the middle of it all, like some ageing hippie relative, is raffish commune Christiania.

# The Sights in a Day

☀ Give into a *kanelsnegle* (cinnamon snail) at **Lagkagehuset** (p80), then burn it off climbing the landmark spiral tower of **Vor Frelsers Kirke** (p77). Your reward is a breathtaking view of the city. From here, it's a gentle walk to **Christiania** (p72), Copenhagen's ramshackle heart of alternative living. Make sure to explore the ramparts at its eastern end, where the air is bucolic and the architecture eclectic.

☀ Lunch harbourside at **Copenhagen Street Food** (p79), then squeeze into Henrik Vibskov's **Den Plettede Gris** (p79) for an arty caffeine fix. Continue north to ponder architect Henning Larsen's controversial **Operaen** (p80). Alternatively, cross back into Christianshavn and check out the exhibition and bookshop at the **Dansk Arkitektur Centre** (p77).

☾ Christianshavn is home to three of the city's top restaurants. Assuming you don't have a reservation at **Noma** (p78), book a table at **Kadeau** (p78) or **Kanalen** (p78), both lauded for their breathtaking New Nordic menus. If it's Wednesday or later in the week, cap the night with live tunes at still-rocking veteran **Loppen** (p74).

## ◉ Top Sights

Christiania (p72)

## ♥ Best of Copenhagen

**Architecture**
Operaen (p80)

**Eating**
Noma (p78)

Kadeau (p78)

Kanalen (p78)

**Outdoor Experiences**
Bastionen + Loven (p79)

Christianshavns Bådudlejning & Café (p80)

## Getting There

Ⓜ **Metro** Christianshavn station sits on Torvegade, Christianshavn's main thoroughfare.

🚍 **Bus** Routes 2A, 40 and 350S cross Christianshavn along Torvegade. Route 9A runs along Torvegade, then along Prinsessegade, passing Christiania and terminating at Operaen on Holmen.

⛴ **Harbour Bus** For Christianshavn, alight commuter ferries at Knippelsbro. For Operaen, alight at Opera.

## Top Sights
# Christiania

Escape the capitalist crunch at Freetown Christiania. Since its establishment by squatters in 1971, this military-barracks-turned-commune has drawn nonconformists from across the globe, attracted by the concept of collective business, workshops and communal living. Explore beyond the area's infamous 'Pusher St' – lined with shady hash and marijuana dealers – and you'll stumble upon an unexpected treasure trove of offbeat DIY homes, *hyggelig* (cosy) gardens, laid-back nosh spots, beer gardens and one of the city's best-loved music venues.

⊙ Map p18; C3

www.christiania.org

Prinsessegade

🚌 2A, 9A, 40, 350S, Ⓜ Christianshavn

Streets of Christiana

# Don't Miss

### Dyssen at Christiania

Dyssen is Christiania's best-kept secret. A long, pencil-thin rampart on the eastern side of the old city moat, it's connected to Christiania's eastern edge by bridge. Running north–south along the rampart is a 2km-long path, studded with beautiful maples and ash, hawthorn, elder and wild cherry trees, not to mention the homes of some rather fortunate Christianites. It's a perfect spot for lazy ambling, slow bike rides or some quiet downtime by the water among the swans, herons, moorhens and coots. Some locals even head here to forage for edible snails. Yet Dyssen has a dark past. The rampart was the site of Denmark's last execution ground, where 29 convicted Nazi sympathisers faced the firing squad following the country's postwar trials. The final execution, taking place in 1950, was of Niels Rasmussen Ib Birkedal Hansen, the most senior Danish member of the Gestapo. Eerily, the concrete floor and drain are still visible by the path at the northern end of Dyssen.

### Stadens Museum for Kunst

Christianites refer to Christiania as 'Staden' (The Town), and the name of art gallery Stadens Museum for Kunst is a tongue-in-cheek play on the more 'establishment' Statens Museum for Kunst. You'll find the place on the 2nd floor of the Loppen building, a former artillery warehouse dating from 1863 and flanking Prinsessegade, just beside Christiania's main entrance. Head up for rotating exhibitions of contemporary art, spanning both local and international artists, and covering anything from drawings and paintings to installations. On any given month you might be poring over Greenlandic stoneware, recycled Tunisian

## ☑ Top Tips

▶ From late June to the end of August, 60- to 90-minute guided tours (Dkr40) of Christiania run daily at 3pm (weekends only September to late June). Tours commence just inside Christiania's main entrance on Prinsessegade.

▶ While taking photos in Christiania is generally fine, do not snap pictures on or around the unsavoury main drag of Pusher St. The area is lined with illegal cannabis dealers who can become nervous or aggressive if photographed.

## ✕ Take a Break

For a cheap and healthy lunch, kick back at vegetarian Morgenstedet (p79). Come dinner, ditch Christiania's so-so restaurant Spiseloppen for nearby Copenhagen Street Food (p79) or upmarket Kanalen (p78).

sculpture or local photography. The gallery also houses a petite cafe for any caffeine-fuelled art debate you may be itching to have.

### Den Grå Hal

The Grey Hall is the commune's largest cultural venue, able to pack in around 1500 people. It was built in 1893, originally as a riding hall for the military. With the establishment of Freetown Christiania, the hall found new purpose as a hub for art and music. Some of the biggest names in music have rocked its weathered walls over the years, among them Bob Dylan, Metallica and Manic Street Preachers. While its calendar is hardly jam-packed these days, the building is worth a look for its architecture and colourful graffiti. In December Den Grå Hal becomes the focal point for Christiania's Christmas festivities, which include a Yuletide market.

### DIY Architecture

Beyond its graffiti-strewn barrack buildings, Christiania is home to some of the city's most eclectic, imaginative architecture. Much of this is in the form of 'tiny houses', small abodes built by hand using salvaged materials. Follow the commune's quieter paths and you'll stumble upon a whimsical collection of buildings, from a home made entirely of random window frames to converted greenhouses, German *bauwagens* (wooden caravans) and Roma wagons, and houses on boats and floating platforms. Many of the most intriguing creations are located beside, or close to, the old city moat on Christiania's eastern side. Needless to say, these are private abodes, so remember to be respectful and considerate.

### Loppen

Its motto might be 'Going out of business since 1973', but 40-something **Loppen** (☏ 32 57 84 22; www.loppen. dk; Bådsmandsstræde 43; ⏱ 8.30pm-late Sun-Thu, 9pm-late Fri & Sat) keeps rocking on. In the same wooden-beamed warehouse as art gallery Stadens Museum for Kunst, this joint has served up some big names in music over the years, among them the Smashing Pumpkins and Animal Collective. It's also a solid venue for lesser-known and emerging talent, both local and international. The music styles are as eclectic as the crowds, with anything from rock, funk and folk to postpunk, dubstep, hip hop and death metal. While gigs generally take place Wednesday to Sunday, it's always a good idea to check the website before heading in. Cash only.

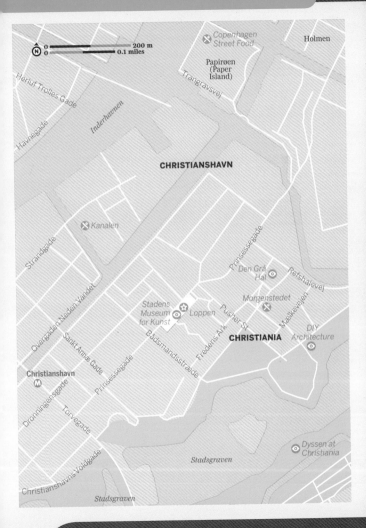

Copenhagen Street Food

Holmen

Papirøen (Paper Island)

Trangravsvej

Herluf Trolles Gade

Inderhavnen

Havnegade

CHRISTIANSHAVN

Kanalen

Strandgade

Prinsessegade

Den Grå Hal

Refshalevej

Morgenstedet

Overgaden Neden Vandet

Stadens Museum for Kunst

Loppen

Pusher St

Mælkevejen

Sankt Anna Gade

Badsmandsstræde

Fredens Ark

CHRISTIANIA

DIY Architecture

Christianshavn Ⓜ

Prinsessegade

Dronningensgade

Torvegade

Stadsgraven

Dyssen at Christiania

Christianshavns Voldgade

Stadsgraven

0 — 200 m
0 — 0.1 miles

NØRREPORT

Kongens Have

NYHAVN

Gothersgade

Store Kongensgade

Bredgade

Sankt Annæ Plads

Amaliehaven

Amalienborg plads

Kvæsthusgraven

Priestræde

Kongens Nytorv

Holmens Kanal

Tordenskjoldsgade

Holmens Bro

Nyhavn

Nyhavn

Nyhavnbro

Sankt Annæ Plads

Kanonbådsvej

Holmen

Dannesk iold-Samsøes Allé

Olfsværftvej

Elværftsvej

Ekvipagemestervej

Halvtolv

Kløvermarksvej

Yderlandsvej

Reffshalevej

Inderhavnen

Ydrehavnen

Papirøen (Paper Island)

Havnegade

Dansk Arkitektur Centre

CHRISTIANSHAVN

Christiania

Prinsessegade

Vor Frelsers Kirke

Bådsmandstræde

Sankt Annæ Gade

Overgaden Oven Vandet

Christianshavn

Christianshavns Voldgade

Dronningensgade

Vermlandsgade

Moelenovej

Christmas Møllers Plads

Stadsgraven

Amager Fælledvej

Stadsgraven

Amager Blvd

Strandgade

Wildersgade

Torvegade

Christians Kirke

Overgaden Neden Vandet

Overgaden

Langebrogade

Langebro

Knippelsbro

Christian IV's Bro

Slotsholmens Kanal

Borgsgade

SLOTSHOLMEN

Christiansborg

Tøjhusgade

Vindebrogade

Frederiksholms Kanal

CHRISTIANS BRYGGE

Christians Brygge

Inderhavnen

Slidshavnen

GoBoat

Havneparken

Islands Brygge

Havnebadet (50m)

200 m
0.1 miles

# Sights

## Vor Frelsers Kirke    CHURCH

1 ⊙ Map p76, C3

It's hard to miss this 17th-century church and its 95m-high spiral tower. For a soul-stirring panoramic city view, make the head-spinning 400-step ascent to the top – the last 150 steps run along the outside rim of the tower, narrowing to the point where they literally disappear at the top. Inspired by Borromini's tower of St Ivo in Rome, the colourful spire was added in 1752 by Lauritz de Thurah. Inside, the church wows with its elaborately carved pipe organ from 1698 and an ornate baroque altar. (www.vorfrelserskirke.dk; Sankt Annæ Gade 29; church free, tower adult/child Dkr40/10; ⊙11am-3.30pm, closed during services, tower 10am-7.15pm Mon-Sat, 10.30am-7.15pm Sun Jun-Sep, reduced hours rest of year; 🚌2A, 9A, 40, 350S, MChristianshavn)

## GoBoat    BOATING

2 ⊙ Map p76, A4

What could be more 'Copenhagen' than sailing around the harbour and canals in your own solar-powered boat? You don't need prior sailing experience and each comes with a built-in picnic table (you can buy supplies at GoBoat or bring your own). Boats seat up to eight and rates are per boat, so the more in your group, the cheaper per person. (📞40 26 10 25; www.goboat.dk; Islands Brygge 10; boat hire 1/3hr Dkr395/999; ⊙10am-sunset; 🚼)

## Dansk Arkitektur Centre    GALLERY

3 ⊙ Map p76, B3

You'll find the Danish Architecture Centre inside Gammel Dok, a 19th-century harbourside warehouse. Aside from an excellent bookshop and pano-ramic cafe, the centre runs changing exhibitions on Danish and interna-tional architecture. On Sundays from May to September, the centre also runs two-hour walking tours of the city (Dkr125). See the website for tour themes and details. (Danish Architecture Centre; 📞32 57 19 30; www.dac.dk; Strand-gade 27B; exhibition adult/child Dkr40/free, 5-9pm Wed free; ⊙exhibition & bookshop 10am-5pm Mon, Tue & Thu-Sun, to 9pm Wed, cafe from 11am Mon-Fri, 10am-4pm Sat & Sun; 🚌2A, 19, 47, 66, 350S, MChristianshavn)

## Overgaden    GALLERY

4 ⊙ Map p76, B3

Rarely visited by tourists, this non-profit art gallery runs about 10 exhibi-tions annually, putting the spotlight on contemporary installation art and pho-tography, usually by younger artists. The gallery also runs a busy calender of artist talks, lectures and film screen-ings. See the website for upcoming events. (📞32 57 72 73; www.overgaden. org; Overgaden Neden Vandet 17; admission free; ⊙1-5pm Tue, Wed & Fri-Sun, to 8pm Thu; 🚌2A, 9A, 40, 350S, MChristianshavn)

## Local Life

### Islands Brygge Havnebadet

Come summer, sun-seeking locals gravitate to **Islands Brygge Havnebadet** (off Map p76; admission free; ☉7am-7pm Mon-Fri, 11am-7pm Sat & Sun Jun-Aug; 👬; ☐5A, 12, Ⓜ Islands Brygge). Copenhagen's architecturally designed outdoor pool complex. Located just south of Christianshavn in Islands Brygge, its combo of pools sits right in Copenhagen's clean, bracing inner harbour. In 2014 plans were under way for winter-friendly saunas and thermal baths, as well as a sixth pool.

### Christians Kirke                    CHURCH

5 ◉ Map p76, B3

Designed by the Danish architect Nicolai Eigtved and completed in 1759, Christians Kirke is well known for its theatrical, rococo interior. The church once served Copenhagen's German congregation. (☑32 54 15 76; Strandgade 1; ☉10am-4pm Tue-Fri; ☐2A, 9A, 40, 350S, Ⓜ Christianshavn)

# Eating

## Noma                    MODERN DANISH $$$

6 ✕ Map p76, C2

Noma is a Holy Grail for gastronomes across the globe. Using Scandinavian-sourced produce such as musk ox and skyr curd, head chef René Redzepi

and his team create extraordinary symphonies of flavour and texture. Tables are booked months ahead, so expect to join the waiting list. Tip: parties of four or more have a better chance of landing a table with shorter notice. (☑32 96 32 97; www.noma.dk; Strandgade 93; degustation menu Dkr1600; ☉noon-4pm & 7pm-12.30am Tue-Sat; ☐2A, 9A, 11A, 40, 66, 350S, Ⓜ Christianshavn)

## Kadeau             MODERN SCANDINAVIAN $$$

7 ✕ Map p76, B3

This is the Michelin-starred sibling of Bornholm's critically acclaimed Kadeau, its outstanding New Nordic cuisine now firmly on the radar of both local and visiting gastronomes. Whether it's salted and burnt scallops drizzled in clam bouillon, or an unexpected combination of toffee, créme fraiche, potatoes, radish and elderflower, dishes are evocative, revelatory and soul-lifting. An equally exciting wine list and sharp, warm service make this place a must. Book ahead. (☑33 25 22 23; www.kadeau.dk; Wildersgade 10A; 4/8-course menu Dkr550/850; ☉noon-3.30pm Wed-Fri & 6pm-late Tue-Sun)

## Kanalen                MODERN DANISH $$$

8 ✕ Map p76, C3

Reborn Kanalen offers an irresistible combination: extraordinary modern Danish food and a canalside location. While the lunch menu delivers competent renditions of Danish classics, it's the dinner menu that takes the breath away. Expect seamless, sophisticated dishes where pillow-soft cod is wrapped in beetroot gel, or where baked plum schmoozes with liquorice and white chocolate sorbet and white chocolate gel and ganache. (📞32 95 13 30; www.restaurant-kanalen.dk; Wilders Plads 2; 6/7-course menu Dkr700/800; ⏰11.30am-3pm & 5.30-10pm Mon-Sat; 🚍2A, 9A, 11A, 40, 66, 350S, Ⓜ Christianshavn)

## Cafe Wilder
INTERNATIONAL $$

9 🍴 Map p76, B3

This corner classic serves beautiful, generous lunch options like hot smoked salmon salad with organic egg, baked tomatoes and rye croutons. Come evening, tuck into reassuring dishes like butter-roasted poussin with creamy portobello mushroom risotto. One of Copenhagen's oldest cafes, the place makes several appearances in the cult TV drama series *Borgen*. (www.cafewilder.dk; Wildersgade 56; lunch Dkr90-149, dinner mains Dkr179-209; ⏰9am-9.30pm Mon-Wed, 9am-10pm Thu & Fri, 11am-10pm Sat, 11am-9.30pm Sun; 🛜; 🚍2A, 9A, 40, 350S, Ⓜ Christianshavn)

## Bastionen + Løven
DANISH $$

10 🍴 Map p76, C4

While the elegant bare wood interior and story-book garden of this old miller's cottage is enough to induce bucolic Nordic fantasies, the reason to head here is the weekend buffet brunch: book one week ahead (it's that popular). The restaurant also serves lunch and dinner, though

both are a hit and miss affair, with significantly better options in the same price range. Cash only. (Christianshavn Voldgade 50; weekend brunch Dkr175, dinner mains Dkr185-215; ⏰11am-9.30pm Tue-Fri, 10am-9.30pm Sat, 10am-2pm Sun; 🛜; 🚍2A, 9A 40, 350S, Ⓜ Christianshavn)

## Morgenstedet
VEGETARIAN $

11 🍴 Map p76, C3

A homely, hippy bolthole in the heart of Christiania, Morgenstedet offers but two dishes of the day, one of which is usually a soup. Choices are always

### ⊙ Local Life
**Papirøen (Paper Island)**

Connected to Christianshavn by bridge, the pocket-sized island of Christiansholm is better known as Papirøen (Paper Island), a reference to its recent past as a newspaper storage facility. Now a hub of postindustrial cool, it's home to **Copenhagen Street Food** (Map p76, C2; wwwcopenhagenstreetfood.dk; Warehouse 7 & 8, Trangravsvej 14, Papirøen; dishes from Dkr40; ⏰food stalls generally noon-10pm; 📷; 🚍11A, 66, ⛴Papirøen), a hangar-style food market packed with artisan food trucks and stalls, bars and hipster baristas. Lazily guarding the entrance to Papirøen is tiny cafe **Den Plettede Gris** (Map p76, C2; Trangravsvej 5; ⏰9.30am-6pm Mon-Fri, 10am-6pm Sat & Sun; 🛜; 🚍9A, ⛴Papirøen), the latest venture for Danish designer, artist, musician and all-round avant-gardiste Henrik Vibskov.

vegetarian and organic, and best devoured in the bucolic bliss of the cafe garden. (www.morgenstedet.dk; Langgaden; mains Dkr80-100; ⏰noon-9pm Tue-Sun; 🍴; 🚌2A, 9A, 40, 350S, Ⓜ️Christianshavn)

### Lagkagehuset

BAKERY $

12 🍽️ Map p76, B3

Right opposite Christianshavn metro station, this is the original (and some would say the best) of the Lagkagehuset bakeries. Handy for a quick bite on the go, its counters heave with luscious pastries, salubrious sandwiches, mini pizzas and heavyweight loaves of rye bread. You'll find a handful of counter seats as well as free wi-fi if you insist on Instagramming your *kanelsnegle*. (📞32 57 36 07; www.lagkagehuset.dk; Torvegade 45; pastries from Dkr18, sandwiches Dkr50; ⏰6am-7pm Sat-Thu, to 7.30pm Fri; 🛜; 🚌2A, 9A, 40, 350S, Ⓜ️Christianshavn)

# Drinking

### Christianshavns Bådudlejning og Café

CAFE, BAR

13 🍺 Map p76, B3

Right on Christianshavn's main canal, this festive, wood-decked cafe-bar is a wonderful spot for drinks by the water. It's a cosy, affable hang-out, with jovial crowds, strung lights and little rowboats (available for hire) docked like bathtime toys. There's grub for the peckish and gas heaters and tarpaulins to ward off any northern chill. (📞32 96 53 53; www.baadudlejningen.dk;

Overgaden Neden Vandet 29; ⏰9am-midnight daily Jun–mid-Aug, reduced hours rest of year, closed Oct-Mar; 🛜; 🚌2A, 9A, 40, 350S, Ⓜ️Christianshavn)

### Kaffi

CAFE

14 🍺 Map p76, A4

A short walk from Langebro and the Islands Brygge waterfront, locally loved Kaffi brews strong, velvety coffee, as well as pouring a small selection of wines, beers and spirits. Free wi-fi, power sockets and amiable staff make it a good spot if you need to tap away on your laptop. On our last visit, food options were limited to pastries. (Vestmannagade 4, Islands Brygge; ⏰8am-3pm Mon & Tue, to 5pm Wed & Thu, to 9pm Fri, 9am-6pm Sat, 9am-3pm Sun; 🛜; 🚌5A, 12, Ⓜ️Islands Brygge)

# Entertainment

### Operaen

OPERA

15 ⭐ Map p76, D1

Designed by the late Henning Larsen, Copenhagen's state-of-the-art opera house has two stages: the Main Stage and the smaller, more experimental Takkeloftet. The repertoire runs the gamut from classic to contemporary opera. Productions usually sell out in advance, so book ahead or you might miss the fat lady singing. (Copenhagen Opera House; 📞box office 33 69 69 69; www.kglteater.dk; Ekvipagemestervej 10; 🚌9A, ⚓Opera)

Understand

# The Danish Table

Food has become one of Copenhagen's strongest selling points in recent years. Not only is it the home to world-famous, chart-topping restaurant Noma, it's the stomping ground of an ever-expanding league of bold, brilliant young chefs turning top produce into groundbreaking innovations and putting new verve into long-loved classics. So grab a (beautifully designed) fork and find a spot at the coveted Danish table.

### New Nordic

Despite some claims of overexposure, Denmark's New Nordic cuisine continues to thrill food critics, editors, bloggers and general gluttons across the globe. A cuisine broadly defined by seasonality, sustainability and a rediscovery of Nordic cooking methods, its colours, flavours and textures distinctly reflect the Scandinavian region. It's a cuisine that has also thrown the spotlight on the region's rarer ingredients, from Greenlandic musk ox to Swedish truffles. While the world's most famous New Nordic restaurant remains Noma (p78), it's by no means the only New Nordic star in town, with other standouts including Michelin-starred Kadeau (p78). Beyond these top-tier cult restaurants, contemporary Danish innovation is also driving a growing number of casual, midrange eateries, from Höst (p94) and Manfreds og Vin (p101) to Kødbyens Fiskebar (p113) and Kadeau's baby brother, Pony (p115).

### Danish Classics

Despite the New Nordic revolution, old-school Danish fare remains a major player on the city's tables. Indeed, tucking into classics such as *frikadeller* (meatballs), *sild* (pickled herring) and Denmark's most famous culinary export, smørrebrød (open sandwiches), at institutions such as Schønnemann (p50) is an integral part of the Copenhagen experience. The basic smørrebrød is a slice of rye bread topped with any number of ingredients, from roast beef or pork to juicy shrimps, pickled herring, liver pâté or fried fish fillet. The garnishes are equally variable, with the sculptured final product often looking too good to eat. In the laws of Danish smørrebrød, smoked salmon is served on white bread, and herring on rye bread. Whatever the combination, the iconic dish is best paired with akvavit and an invigorating beer.

Explore

# Nørreport

Wedged between the city centre and the central lakes, Nørreport and its surrounds are a delicious blend of market stalls, restaurants, bars, and distinguished art collections. You'll find drool-inducing market Torvehallerne KBH and the quietly hip strip of Nansensgade, not to mention several flagship cultural sights. Topping it off is the restorative green of Botanisk Have and Kongens Have.

# The Sights in a Day

☼ Breakfast at **Torvehallerne KBH** (p90), slurping espresso at **Coffee Collective** (p90) and oats at **Grød** (p90). While both these stalls open early, most of the market vendors open at 10am (11am on Sunday), so time your visit for a postbreakfast market saunter. Cross tranquil **Botanisk Have** (p93) on your way to **Statens Museum for Kunst** (p88), where many of the country's greatest masterpieces await.

☼ Close by is **Aamanns Takeaway** (p96), justifiably famous for its contemporary take on smørrebrød (open sandwiches). Mouth wiped, feel the romance with a stroll through **Kongens Have** (p87) on your way to **Rosenborg Slot** (p84), former royal summer pad and home to the crown jewels. Dazzling assets are also in abundance at nearby **Davids Samling** (p93), known for its superlative hoard of Islamic decorative arts.

☾ Come evening, opt for low-key cool on bar-sprinkled Nansensgade. Oenophiles will swoon at the choice of wines at **Bibendum** (p97), while fans of kooky interiors will feel right at home at offbeat **Bankeråt** (p97). For a thrilling, affordable New Nordic dinner, book a table at **Höst** (p94).

For a local's day in Nørreport, see p90.

## ◉ Top Sights

Rosenborg Slot (p84)

Statens Museum for Kunst (p88)

## ◯ Local Life

To Market, To Market (p90)

## ♥ Best of Copenhagen

**Museums**

Rosenborg Slot (p84)

Statens Museum for Kunst (p88)

Davids Samling (p93)

Hirschsprung (p94)

**Eating**

Höst (p94)

Orangeriet (p94)

Aamanns Takeaway (p96)

## Getting There

Ⓜ **Metro & S-Train** Just by Torvehallerne KBH, Nørreport station serves both metro and S-train services.

🚍 **Bus** Nørreport station is also a major hub for city buses. Routes 6A, 42, 184 and 185 pass by Rosenborg Slot, Botanisk Have and Statens Museum for Kunst. Route 11A runs along Gothersgade, passing Kongens Have and Cinemateket.

## Top Sights
# Rosenborg Slot

Rosenborg Slot is one of Copenhagen's greatest landmarks: a moated, turreted castle graced with blue-blooded portraits and tapestries, royal hand-me-downs and top-tier bling. Built between 1606 and 1633 by Christian IV to serve as his summer home, the building would be later mainly used for official functions, as well as to safeguard the monarchy's heirlooms. In the 1830s the Danish royals opened the castle as a museum, while still using it as as their own giant jewellery box. It serves both functions to this day.

◉ Map p18; D2

Øster Voldgade 4A

adult/child Dkr90/free, incl Amalienborg Slot Dkr125/free

⊙ 10am-5pm daily Jun-Aug, 10am-4pm daily May, Sep & Oct, reduced hours rest of year

🚌 6A, 11A, 42, 150S, 173E, 184, 185, 350S, Ⓜ Nørreport

# Don't Miss

### Christian IV's Winter Room

Room 1 is the original building's best-preserved room. The rich wooden panelling – adorned with inlaid Dutch paintings – was begun by Court cabinetmaker Gregor Greuss and completed in 1620. Adorning the ceiling are mythological paintings by Danish-born Dutch painter Pieter Isaacsz, the works replacing the room's original stucco ceiling c 1770. Among the room's items is a 17th-century Florentine tabletop, made of inlaid semiprecious stones. Equally fascinating is the Astronomical Clock, which comes with moving figures and musical works. Dating back to 1594, the timepiece was made by the renowned Swiss clockmaker Isaac Habrecht.

### Christian IV's Bedroom

It's in room 3 that Denmark's famous 'Builder King', Christian IV, died on 28 February 1648, and it's here that you'll find his nightcap and slippers, as well as the bloodstained clothes from his naval battle of Kolberger Heide in July 1644. The walls, doors and stucco ceiling all date back to Christian IV's time, as does the stucco ceiling in the adjoining toilet. The toilet's fetching blue and white wall tiles date to Frederik IV's refurbishment of the castle in 1705. Some of the tiles are the Dutch original, while others were made in Copenhagen in 1736. Back in the day, a water cistern was used for flushing, with the king's business expelled straight into the moat.

### Mirror Cabinet

It mightn't be the 1st floor's most lavish room, but the Mirror Cabinet is certainly its most curious. Inspired by France's Palace of Versailles, the room's mirrored ceiling, floor and walls would

☑ **Top Tips**

▶ While information panels are scarce, smartphone users with a scanner app can download information about the collection's highlights via the exhibition barcodes. If you don't have a smartphone – or if you simply want more extensive coverage of the collection – catalogues are available at the ticket office, either for hire (Dkr10) or purchase (Dkr25).

✕ **Take a Break**

On the other side of Kongens Have (p96) is a good spot to grab a freshly made sandwich and coffee to enjoy in the park. For something more upscale, book a table at gorgeous Orangeriet (p94), also on the east side of the park.

sit comfortably on the pages of a 1970s interior design magazine. In reality, the interior is pure baroque, dating back to the beginning of the 18th century and specially designed for Frederik IV. All the rage at the time, mirror cabinets were commonly featured in the innermost sanctum of a king's suite, usually in connection with the royal bedchamber. Frederik IV's bedchamber was downstairs in room 4, a spiral staircase connecting it to the Mirror Cabinet. If the thought of all these mirrors seems a little kinky, bear in mind that the adjoining room is where the king kept his collection of erotica.

### Knights' Hall

Originally a ballroom, the Knights' Hall was completed in 1624 and the last of the castle's rooms to be furnished. Gracing the walls are the Rosenborg Tapestries, 12 woven works depicting the battles between Denmark and Sweden during the Scanian War (1675–79). The tapestries were a PR exercise of sorts, commissioned by Christian V to flaunt his military prowess. The Knights' Hall is also home to the coronation thrones and a stucco ceiling with four paintings by Hendrick Krock that represent the four regalia: crown, orb, sword and sceptre. Two small chambers run off the hall, one displaying Venetian glassware, the other home to Royal Copenhagen Porcelain's original Flora Danica set, adorned with exquisite botanical motifs.

### Basement Cellar Rooms & Green Room

Rosenborg Slot's undisputed pièce de résistance is its basement, home to an extraordinary collection of royal regalia and gifts. Some of the dusty bottles in the castle cellar date back to the 18th century. The wine is still used on special royal occasions, though it's now merely splashed into more palatable drops as a ceremonial gesture. The northernmost cellar room contains some rather unusual decorative objects, including an 18th-century chandelier made of amber by Lorenz Spengler. At the southern end of the basement is the Green Room, itself laden with intriguing royal paraphernalia. Keep an eye out for Christian IV's riding trappings, used at his coronation in 1596.

### Treasury

Just off the Green Room, the Treasury is where you'll find the castle's most valuable treasures. These include Christian IV's spectacular crown, created especially for his coronation by Dirich Fyring in Odense. Made of gold, pearls and table-cut stones and weighing 2.89kg, its features include the figure of a self-pecking pelican feeding its offspring blood; a symbolic representation of the need for rulers to willingly sacrifice their own blood for their subjects. Other show-stoppers include the jewel-studded sword of Christian III (crafted in 1551) and the obsessively detailed Oldenburg Horn. Made of silver in the mid-15th century, the horn

Hans Christian Andersen statue by August Saabye

is believed to have been a gift from Christian I to Cologne's cathedral. The gift found itself in Danish hands once more after the Reformation.

## Kongens Have

Fronting Rosenborg Slot is much-loved Kongens Have (King's Garden). The city's oldest park, it was laid out in the early 17th century by Christian IV, who used it as his vegetable patch.

These days it has a little more to offer, including immaculate flower beds, romantic garden paths and a mario-nette theatre with free performances during the summer season (2pm and 3pm Tuesday to Sunday). Located on the northeastern side of the park, the theatre occupies one of the neoclas-sical pavilions designed by Danish architect Peter Meyn.

## Top Sights
# Statens Museum for Kunst

Home to almost 9000 paintings and sculptures, and around 300,000 works of art on paper, the National Gallery of Denmark is the country's pre-eminent art institution. The gallery's collection spans centuries of creative expression, from 14th-century Sienese altarpieces to 21st-century Danish installations. You'll find no shortage of Danish greats, including Golden Age icons such as Christoffer Wilhelm Eckersberg and Christen Købke, 20th-century mavericks Asger Jorn and Per Kirkeby and current innovators like Elmgreen & Dragset.

◉ Map 92; D1

www.smk.dk

Sølvgade 48-50

special exhibitions adult/child Dkr110/free

⊙ 10am-5pm Tue & Thu-Sun, to 8pm Wed

🚌 6A, 26, 42, 173E, 184, 185

# Don't Miss

### Danish & Nordic Art 1750–1900

Statens Museum's collection of Scandinavian art includes several works by Norwegian artist Edvard Munch, as well as an impressive compilation of 19th-century Danish masters. Don't miss the raw rage of Nicolai Abildgaard's *Wounded Philoctetes* (1775), Johan Christian Dahl's deeply atmospheric *Winter Landscape near Vordingborg, Denmark* (1829) and Joakim Skovgaard's monumental *Christ in the Realm of the Dead* (1891–94).

### French Art 1900–30

The gallery's collection of 20th-century 'Paris-scene' artworks includes creations by Georges Braque and Pablo Picasso. André Derain's *Woman in a Chemise* (1906) is a highlight from the artist's Fauvist period, and a striking contrast to his sombre *Two Sisters* (1914). Also notable are the numerous works by Henri Matisse, including *Interior with a Violin* (1918) and *Portrait of Madame Matisse* (1905), also known as *The Green Line*. The latter is considered a masterpiece of modern portrait painting.

### Danish & International Art after 1900

The Danish works here are especially notable, among them expressionist painter Jens Søndergaard's brooding *Stormy Sea* (1954) and CoBrA artists such as Asger Jorn. Look out for Bjørn Nørgaard's infamous *The Horse Sacrifice* and *Objects from the Horse Sacrifice*, which document the artist's ritualistic sacrifice of a horse in 1970 to protest the Vietnam War.

## ☑ Top Tips

▶ On three Fridays in spring and three Fridays in autumn, the National Gallery stays open late for its pop-up party, SMK Fridays. The free event includes food, art talks, DJs and creative workshops. Check the website for upcoming dates.

## ✗ Take a Break

When museum fatigue kicks in, retreat to the National Gallery's bright, geometric cafe, created by designer Peter Lassen and artist Bjørn Nørgaard. An easy 450m east of the National Gallery, Aamanns Takeaway (p96) serves excellent smørrebrød.

# Local Life
## To Market, To Market

An ode to the fresh, the tasty and the slow, food market **Torvehallerne KBH** (www.torvehallernekbh.dk; ⏱10am-7pm Mon-Thu, to 8pm Fri, to 6pm Sat, 11am-5pm Sun) peddles everything from seasonal herbs and berries, to smoked meats, seafood and cheeses, smørrebrød, fresh pasta, and coffee. You could easily spend an hour or more exploring its twin glass halls, chatting to the vendors, stocking the larder and noshing on freshly cooked sit-down meals.

### ❶ Grød
Holistic **Grød** (hall 2, stall A8; porridge Dkr40-75; ⏱8am-7pm Mon-Thu, to 8pm Fri, 10am-6pm Sat, 10am-5pm Sun) turns stodge sexy with its modern take on porridge. Made-from-scratch options might include porridge with gooseberry compote, liquorice sugar, skyr (Icelandic yoghurt) and hazelnuts, or healthier-than-thou grain porridge cooked in carrot juice and served with apple, roasted flaxseeds, raisins and a zingy ginger syrup. If it's later in the day, try the chicken congee.

### ❷ Coffee Collective
Save your caffeine fix for **Coffee Collective** (www.coffeecollective.dk; hall 2, stall C1; ⏱7am-8pm Mon-Fri, 8am-6pm Sat & Sun). The beans here are sourced ethically and directly from farmers, and the team usually offers two espresso blends: one full-bodied and traditional, the other more stringent and Third Wave in flavour. If espresso is just too passé, order a hand-brewed cup from the Kalita Wave dripper.

### ❸ Omegn
Nordic deli **Omegn** (hall 1, stall E2; cheese & charcuterie platter Dkr70-95; ⏱9am-7pm Mon-Thu, to 8pm Fri, to 6pm Sat, 10am-5pm Sun) stocks the top products from various small-scale Danish farms and food artisans. The cheese selection includes Thybo, a sharp cow's milk cheese from northern Jutland. Peckish punters can nibble on the cheese and charcuterie platter or go old-school with a warming serve of *skipperlabskov* (beef stew).

### ❹ Unika
Arla is one of Denmark's mega dairy companies, and **Unika by Arla** (hall 1, stall F5; ⏱10am-7pm Mon-Thu, to 8pm Fri, to 6pm Sat, 11am-5pm Sun) is its boutique offshoot. The company works with small dairies, artisan cheesemakers and top chefs to produce Nordic-inspired cheeses. Look out for the unpasteurised Kry, which delivers a flavour considered superior to pasteurised cheeses. Equally unique are

# TORVEHALLERNE

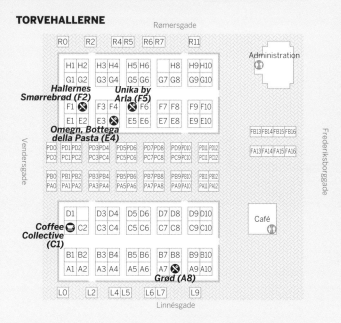

the apple-based dessert wines from Jutland's Cold Hand Winery.

## ❺ Hallernes Smørrebrød

Not only is the smørrebrød scrumptious at **Hallernes Smørrebrød** (hall 1, stall F2; smørrebrød Dkr38-52; ☺10am-7pm Mon-Thu, to 8pm Fri, to 6pm Sat, 11am-5pm Sun), it – like the beers and snaps on offer – is well priced. Grab a spot at the wooden bar, order a Mikkeller beer, and tuck into beautifully presented classics like *fiskefilet* (fish fillet) with remoulade.

## ❻ Bottega della Pasta

While we prefer to focus on Torvelhallerne's Nordic deliciousness, we willingly make a concession for **Bottega della Pasta** (hall 1, stall E4; pasta Dkr80-110; ☺10am-7pm Mon-Thu, to 8pm Fri, to 6pm Sat, 11am-5pm Sun). It's a rocking slice of Italy, where the pasta is made from scratch and turned into insanely fine dishes like rich, earthy pasta with Parmigiano cream and freshly shaved truffle. Bonus points go to the perfectly quaffable house vino.

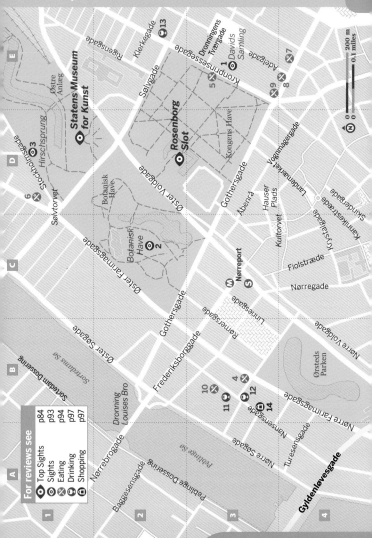

200 m
0.1 miles

For reviews see
| | |
|---|---|
| ◆ Top Sights | p84 |
| ◆ Sights | p93 |
| ✕ Eating | p94 |
| ◑ Drinking | p97 |
| ⊞ Shopping | p97 |

Statens Museum for Kunst

Rosenborg Slot

Botanisk Have

Davids Samling

Nørreport

Ørsteds Parken

Gyldenløvesgade

FOTOVOYAGER/GETTY IMAGES ©

Palmehus, Botanisk Have

# Sights

## Davids Samling
MUSEUM

1  Map p92, E3

Davids Samling is a wonderful curiosity of a gallery housing Scandinavia's largest collections of Islamic art, including jewellery, ceramics and silk, and exquisite works such as an Egyptian rock crystal jug from AD 1000 and a 500-year-old Indian dagger inlaid with rubies. Plus an elegant selection of Danish, Dutch, English and French art, porcelain, silverware and furniture from the 17th to 19th centuries. (☏33 73 49 49; www.davidmus.dk; Kronprinsessegade 30; admission free; ◷10am-5pm Tue & Thu-Sun, to 9pm Wed; ▣1A, 11, 15, 26, 350S)

## Botanisk Have
GARDENS

2  Map p92, C2

Restorative and romantic, Copenhagen's Botanical Garden lays claim to the largest collection of living plants in Denmark. You can amble along tranquil trails punctuated with quotes from Danish poets and writers (in Danish), escape to warmer climes in the 19th-century **Palmehus** (◷10am-3pm May-Sep, closed Mon Oct-Apr) glasshouse, and even pick up honey made using the garden's own bees at the gorgeous little **gift shop** (◷10am-5pm Apr-Sep, to 3.30pm Tue-Sun rest of year). At the garden's northwest corner lies the old-fashioned **Geologisk Museum** (Geology Museum; Øster Voldgade 5-7; adult/child Dkr40/free;

⊙10am-1pm Tue-Fri, 1-4pm Sat & Sun), worth a trip for its exhibition of botanical drawings, dazzling mineral displays and riotously colourful staircase mural by revered Danish artist Per Kirkeby. (Botanical Garden; www.botanik.snm.ku.dk; main entrance Gothersgade 140; ⊙8.30am-6pm daily May-Sep, 8.30am-4pm Tue-Sun Oct-Apr; 👤; 🚌6A, 11A, 14, 40, 42, 150S, 173E, 184, 185, Ⓜ Nørreport, Ⓡ S-train Nørreport)

## Hirschsprung
MUSEUM

3 ◉ Map p92, D1

Dedicated to Danish art of the 19th and early 20th centuries, Den Hirschsprungske Samling is a little jewel-box of a gallery, full of wonderful surprises for art lovers unfamiliar with the classic era of Danish oil painting. Originally the private holdings of tobacco magnate Heinrich Hirschsprung, the museum contains works by 'Golden Age' painters such as Christen Købke and CW Eckersberg, a notable selection by

---

☑ Top Tip
### Picnic in the Park

In the warmer months, few things beat a picnic in Kongens Have or Botanisk Have. Both are within walking distance of Torvehallerne KBH, where you can happily fill your hamper with just-baked bread and pastries, local cheeses and charcuterie, fruits, vegetables and ready-to-eat dishes. Alfresco perfection.

---

Skagen painters PS Krøyer and Anna and Michael Ancher, and also works by the Danish symbolists and the Funen painters. (📞35 42 03 36; www.hirschsprung.dk; Stockholmsgade 20; adult/child Dkr75/free, Wed free; ⊙11am-4pm Tue-Sun; 🚌6A, 14, 40, 42, 43, 150S)

# Eating

## Höst
MODERN DANISH $$

4 🍴 Map p92, B3

Höst's phenomenal popularity is a no-brainer: warm, award-winning interiors, mere-mortal prices and New Nordic food that's equally fabulous and filling. The set menu is great value, with three smaller 'surprise dishes' thrown in, and evocative creations like salted Faroe Islands scallops with corn, raw plums, pickled black trumpet mushrooms and wild garlic. The 'deluxe' wine menu is significantly better than the standard option. Book ahead, especially later in the week. (📞89 93 84 09; www.cofoco.dk; Nørre Farimagsgade 41; mains Dkr195-215, 3-course set menu Dkr295; ⊙5.30-9.30pm daily; 🚌40, Ⓜ Nørrebro)

## Orangeriet
MODERN DANISH $$

5 🍴 Map p92, E3

Take a vintage conservatory, add elegant seasonal menus, and you have Orangeriet. Skirting the eastern edge of Kongens Have, its main man is award-winning chef Jasper Kure, whose contemporary creations focus on sim-

## Understand

### Danish Art: A Primer

Copenhagen is a cultured creature, home to the Royal Danish Academy of Fine Arts and many of Scandinavia's most important art museums, galleries and artists.

#### Current Creatives

Danish artists enjoying international acclaim include conceptual artist Jeppe Hein, duo Elmgreen & Dragset, and Danish-Icelandic Olafur Eliasson, the latter best known for his Weather Project installation in London's Tate Modern, his temporary 'waterfalls' along New York's East River, and his multicoloured walkway atop the ARoS gallery in Aarhus. These artists are represented in several of Copenhagen's major art museums, including Statens Museum for Kunst (p88) and Louisiana (p120).

#### The Golden Age

Some refer to the present day as the new 'Golden Age' of Danish art, looking to the first half of the 19th century when artists such as Christoffer Eckersberg (1783–1853) and Christen Købke (1810–48) painted scenes of everyday life with startling clarity and power. You'll find numerous paintings from this period at Statens Museum for Kunst (p88) and Hirschsprung. Ny Carlsberg Glyptotek (p31) also houses art from this period. The leading sculptor of the day was Bertel Thorvaldsen (1770–1844), who spent most of his working life in Rome producing works inspired by classical antiquity. His work features at Thorvaldsens Museum (p41).

#### A Rebellious CoBrA

Another important art movement that evolved in the Danish capital was the CoBrA – an acronym from Copenhagen, Brussels and Amsterdam, the three cities from which the movement's artists originated. Formed in 1948 its founders included Danish abstract artist Asger Jorn (1914–73), a painter, ceramist, printmaker, sculptor and writer. Jorn rebelled against the rules of the art academies, favouring a more spontaneous, unruly approach to creativity and a greater experimentation with materials. This rebellion would result in works exploding with colour, immediacy and fantastical imagery.

plicity and premium produce. Savour the brilliance in clean, intriguing dishes like rimmed cod with celeriac, cabbage, cress and clam sauce with smoked cod roe. Lunch is a simple affair of smørrebrød. Book ahead. (☑33 11 13 07; www.restaurant-orangeriet.dk; Kronprinsessegade 13; smørrebrod Dkr75, 3-/5-course dinner Dkr375/495; ◷11.30am-3pm & 6-10pm Mon-Sat, noon-4pm Sun; ☐11A, 26, 350S)

### Aamanns Takeaway DANISH $$

8 ✕ Map p92, D1

Clued-up foodies get their contemporary smørrebrød fix at Aamanns, where open sandwiches are seasonal, artful and served on Aamanns' own organic sourdough bread (head in before 1pm to avoid waiting). The star option is the beef loin tartare, served with mushroom emulsion, gherkin, pickled beech mushrooms, shallots and mini-potato chips. On weekdays, two simple dinner dishes are also served, one option always being meatballs. (☑35 55 33 44; www.aamanns.dk; Øster Farimagsgade 10; smørrebrød Dkr55-95, dinner mains Dkr90-98; ◷smørrebrød 11am-4pm Mon-Sat, noon-4pm Sun, dinner 5-8pm Mon-Fri; ☐6A, 14, 40, 42, 150S, 184, 185)

### Atelier September CAFE $

7 ✕ Map p92, E4

It might look like a *Vogue* photo shoot with its white-on-white interior, black-clad staff and impossibly beautiful clientele, but Atelier September is very a much a cafe. Kitted out with art, erudite magazines and colourful crockery, it peddles gorgeous espresso and a short list of simple, inspired edibles. Standouts include sliced avocado on rye bread topped with lemon zest, chives, paprika and peppery olive oil. (www.atelier-september.dk; Gothersgade 30; dishes Dkr30-125; ◷8am-6pm Mon-Sat; ☎; ☐11A, Ⓜ Kongens Nytorv)

### Bistro Pastis FRENCH $$

8 ✕ Map p92, E4

Paging both Paris and NYC with its lipstick-red banquettes and white subway tiles, upbeat Pastis is just the ticket for a post-shopping Gallic bite or a more substantial dinner date. Feel fancy over a light *salade chévre chaud* (grilled goat's cheese salad with pickled walnuts and raisins) or delve into warming classics like bouillabaisse (fish soup with Gruyère cheese). (☑33 93 44 11; www.bistro-pastis.dk; Gothersgade 52; salads & sandwiches Dkr115-145, mains Dkr165-285; ◷11.30am-3pm & 5.30-10.30pm Mon-Sat; ☐11A, 350S)

### Big Apple SANDWICHES $

9 ✕ Map p92, E3

Concrete floors, rustic communal tables and splashes of vibrant green keep things Nordic and natural at this popular sandwich peddler. The bread is vegan, toasted and stuffed with combos like goat's cheese, avocado, cucumber and homemade pesto. Liquids include freshly squeezed juices and fantastic coffee from top local roastery the Coffee Collective. *And* they have soy milk! (Kronprinsessegade 2; sandwiches Dkr50, salads Dkr55; ◷8am-6pm Mon-Fri, 9am-6pm Sat & Sun; ☎; ☐11A, Ⓜ Kongens Nytorv)

### Sticks 'N' Sushi JAPANESE $$

10 Map p92, B3

The original and still the sexiest contemporary sushi place in Copenhagen, with especially good tuna tartare and hamachi carpaccio options. Other branches crop up in various areas of the city. (☎33 11 14 07; www.sushi.dk; Nansensgade 47; nigiri per piece from Dkr21, sushi & sashimi sets from Dkr105; ☺11am-10pm Sun-Thu, to 10.30pm Fri & Sat; ☐5A, 40, 350S, Ⓜ Nørreport)

# Drinking

### Bibendum WINE BAR

11 Map p92, B3

Cosily set in a rustic cellar on trendy Nansensgade, Bibendum is an oenophile's best friend. Dive in and drool over a savvy list that offers over 30 wines by the glass. The vibe is intimate but relaxed, and the menu of small plates (Dkr89 to Dkr95) simply gorgeous. (Nansensgade 45; ☺4pm-midnight Mon-Sat; 📶; ☐5A, 40, 350S, Ⓜ Nørreport)

### Bankeråt BAR

12 Map p92, B3

A snug spot to get stuffed (literally), kooky, attitude-free Bankeråt is pimped with taxidermic animals in outlandish get-ups – yes, there's even a ram in period costume. The man behind it all is local artist Phillip Jensen. But is it art? Debate this, and the mouth-shaped urinals, over a Carlsberg or

three. (☎33 93 69 88; www.bankeraat.dk; Ahlefeldtsgade 27; ☺9.30am-midnight Mon-Fri, 10.30am-midnight Sat, 10.30am-11pm Sun; 📶; ☐12, 40, 66, 68, Ⓜ Nørrebro)

### Culture Box CLUB

13 Map p92, E2

Electronica connoisseurs swarm to Culture Box, known for its impressive local and international DJ line-ups and sharp sessions of electro, techno, house and drum'n'bass. The club is divided into three spaces: pre-clubbing bar White Box, intimate club space Red Box and heavyweight Black Box, where big-name DJs play the massive sound system. (www.culture-box.com; Kronprinsessegade 54A; ☺White Box 9pm-late Fri & Sat, Red Box 10pm-late Fri & Sat, Black Box midnight-late Fri & Sat; ☐26)

# Shopping

### Piet Breinholm – The Last Bag LEATHER GOODS

14 Map p92, B3

Musician-turned-designer Piet Breinholm is famous for his classic leather satchels, available in small or large, and in colours ranging from sensible black to outrageous canary yellow. A handful of other styles are also available, all using high-quality leather sourced from an ecofriendly Brazilian tannery. Samples and faulty goods are sometimes slashed to half-price. (www.pietbreinholm. dk; Nansensgade 48; ☺11am-7pm Fri, by appointment rest of week; ☐40, Ⓜ Nørreport)

Explore

# Nørrebro

Nørrebro subverts the pristine Nordic stereotype with its dense, sexy funk of 19th-century tenements, street art and multicultural locals. This is one of Copenhagen's most vibrant neighbourhoods, jammed with design studios and boutiques, indie cafes, cult-status restaurants and thumping late-night bars. It's also home to the strangely bewitching cemetery Assistens Kirkegård.

## The Sights in a Day

☀️ Ease into the Nørrebro groove at **Laundromat Cafe** (p102), a lovingly worn hang-out and laundromat rolled into one. People-watch over breakfast or coffee, then boutique-hop the surrounding streets. If it's Saturday, treasure hunt at nearby flea market **Nørrebro Loppemarked** (p103).

☀️ Escape to **Assistens Kirkegård** (p101) and seek out the graves of writer Hans Christian Andersen and Golden Age artists Christoffer Wilhelm Eckersberg and Christen Købke. The cemetery is one of the city's most inviting green spaces, and a popular sunbathing spot in the summer. Lunch on regional grub at **Manfreds og Vin** (p101), then hop the Jægersborggade's booty of artisan studios and fashion boutiques.

🌙 As evening descends, dive into good-time **Kassen** (p103) for happy-hour cocktail specials, then get those fingers dirty at **Oysters & Grill** (p101) – always a good idea to book ahead. If you feel like kicking on, head to of-the-moment Ravnsborggade, a street packed with bustling bars. Among them is the supremely sultry **Kind of Blue** (p102).

 **Best of Copenhagen**

**Eating**
Manfreds og Vin (p101)

Oysters & Grill (p101)

**Drinking**
Coffee Collective (p102)

Nørrebro Bryghus (p102)

**Outdoor Experiences**
Assistens Kirkegård (p101)

## Getting There

🚌 **Bus** Routes 3A, 5A and 350S run along Nørrebrogade, the neighbourhood's main thoroughfare.

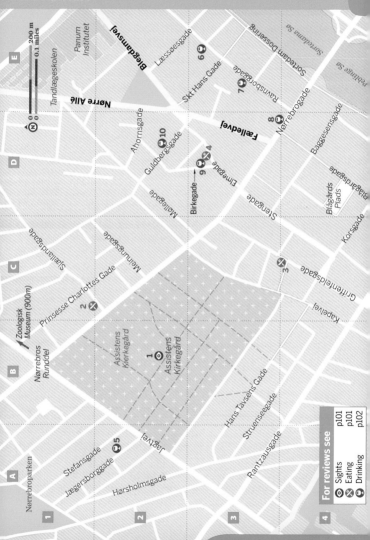

# Sights

## Assistens Kirkegård     CEMETERY

1 ◉ Map p100, B2

You'll find some of Denmark's most celebrated citizens at this famous cemetery, including philosopher Søren Kierkegaard, physicist Niels Bohr, author Hans Christian Andersen and artists Jens Juel, Christen Købke and CW Eckersberg. It's a wonderfully atmospheric place to wander around – as much a park and garden as it is a graveyard. A good place to start is at the main entrance on Kapelvej, which has an office (10am to 4pm weekdays) where you can pick up a brochure mapping famous grave sites. (✆35 37 19 17; http://assistens.dk; Kapelvej 4; ⏰7am-10pm Apr-Sep, to 7pm Oct-Mar; 🚌5A, 350S)

# Eating

## Oysters & Grill     SEAFOOD $$

2 ✖ Map p100, C1

Finger-licking surf and turf is what you get at this rocking, unpretentious classic, complete with kitsch vinyl tablecloths and a fun, casual vibe. If you're a seafood fan, make sure your order includes both the ridiculously fresh oysters and the common cockles drizzled with parsley oil. Meat lovers won't be disappointed either, with cuts that are lust-inducingly tender and succulent. Book ahead. (✆70 20 61 71; cofoco.dk/en/restaurants/oysters-and-grill; Sjællandsgade 1B; mains Dkr155-195;

⏰5.30-9.30pm Mon-Thu, to 10pm Fri & Sat, to 9.15pm Sun; 🛜; 🚌5A)

## Pop – et Spiseri     ITALIAN $$$

3 ✖ Map p100, C4

Petite Pop is run by four Danish women passionate about Italian nosh. There's no conventional menu, just the one four-course menu with matching wines and coffee for Dkr600. Whether it's *pappa al pomodoro* (Tuscan bread soup) or succulent pork with pan-fried Swiss chard, chanterelle mushrooms and rosemary, expect prized produce

## ◯ Local Life
## Manfreds og Vin

Convivial **Manfreds og Vin** (Map p100, A1; ✆36 96 65 93; www.manfreds.dk; Jægersborggade 40; small plates Dkr75-95, 7-course tasting menu Dkr250; ⏰noon-3.30pm & 5.30-10pm; 🛜🞕; 🚌5A, 18, 350S) is the ultimate local bistro, where the provenance of the day's produce is marked on a map of Denmark, where the staffers swill and test wines with genuine passion, and where locals head on their way home from work. The menu favours organic produce, cooked simply and sensationally. Swoon over nuanced, textured dishes like sautéed spinach with lard-roasted croutons and warm poached egg, or slightly charred broccoli served with cream cheese, pickled onion and toasted bulgar wheat. If we could, we'd move in.

and dishes that sing with flavour. Service is knowledgeable and empty wine glasses generously refilled. ( ☑ 42 36 02 22; www.pop-etspiseri.dk; Griffenfeldsgade 28; set menu Dkr600; ⏱ 6-10pm Wed-Fri; 🛜; ☐ 3A, 5A, 350S, 12, 66)

### Laundromat Cafe    INTERNATIONAL $$

4 ✖ Map p100, D3

Cafe, bookstore and laundrette in one, this retrolicious Nørrebro institution is never short of a crowd. It's an especially popular brunch spot, with both 'clean' (vegetarian) and 'dirty' (carnivorous) brunch platters, strong coffee and fresh juices. Breakfast options include porridge and *croque-madame*, while all-day comforters include hamburgers (veggie option included), chilli con carne, and a pear and goat's cheese salad. (www.thelaundromatcafe.com; Elmegade 15; dishes Dkr45-155; ⏱ 8am-midnight Mon-Fri, 10am-midnight Sat & Sun; 🛜; ☐ 3A, 5A, 350S)

# Drinking

### Coffee Collective    CAFE

5 ☕ Map p100, A2

In a city where lacklustre coffee is as common as perfect cheekbones, this micro-roastery peddles the good stuff: we're talking rich, complex cups of caffeinated magic. The baristas are passionate about their beans and the cafe itself sits on creative Jægersborggade in Nørrebro. There are two other outlets, at food market Torvehallerne

KBH (p90) and in Frederiksberg. (www.coffeecollective.dk; Jægersborggade 10; ⏱ 7am-7pm Mon-Fri, 8am-7pm Sat & Sun; ☐ 18, 12, 66)

### Nørrebro Bryghus    BREWERY

6 ☕ Map p100, E3

This now-classic brewery kick-started the microbrewing craze a few years back. Thankfully, the concept remains as alluring as ever, and the place remains a great place to wash down local suds. Rumbling bellies are also accounted for, with the brewery's in-house restaurant serving up tasty, reasonably priced grub like pan-roasted scallops, fish and chips, and risotto. ( ☑ 38 60 38 60; www.noerrebro-bryghus.dk; Ryesgade 3; ⏱ 11am-midnight Mon-Thu, to 2am Fri & Sat; ☐ 3A, 5A, 350S)

### Kind of Blue    BAR

7 ☕ Map p100, E3

Chandeliers, heady perfume and walls painted a hypnotic 1950s blue: the spirit of the Deep South runs deep at intimate Kind of Blue. Named after the Miles Davis album, it's never short of a late-night, hipster crowd, kicking back porters and drinking in owner Claus' personal collection of soul-stirring jazz, blues and folk. You'll find it on Nørrebro's bar-packed Ravnsborggade. ( ☑ 26 35 10 56; www.kindofblue.dk; Ravnsborggade 17; ⏱ 4pm-midnight Mon-Wed, to 2am Thu-Sat; 🛜; ☐ 5A)

## Kassen

BAR

8 Map p100, D3

Loud, sticky Kassen sends livers packing with its dirt-cheap drinks and happy-hour specials (Dkr80 cocktails, anyone?). Dkr250 gets you unlimited drinks on Wednesdays, with two-for-one deals running the rest of the week: all night Thursdays, 2pm to 10pm Fridays, and 8pm to 10pm Saturday. Cocktail choices are stock-standard and a little sweet, but all is forgiven with all that change in your pocket. (Nørrebrogade 18B; ⊙8pm-2am Wed, 8pm-3am Thu, 2pm-4am Fri, 8pm-4am Sat; ⊟5A)

## Malbeck

WINE BAR

9 Map p100, D3

Giant industrial lamps, découpage tabletops and a convivial buzz set the scene at this respected Nørrebro wine bar. Look out for lesser-known Argentine drops, and toast twice to the half-price deals on glasses of vino between 4pm and 6pm Sunday to Thursday. If hunger washes over, graze on the likes of cheese, charcuterie and croquettes, or tuck into the juicy slab of steak. (Birkegade 2; ⊙4pm-midnight Sun-Thu, to 1am Fri & Sat; ⊟3A, 5A, 350S)

## Rust

CLUB, LIVE MUSIC

10 Map p100, D2

A smashing place attracting one of the largest, coolest crowds in Copenhagen. Live acts focus on alternative or upcoming indie rock, hiphop or electronica, while the club churns out hip hop, dancehall and electro on Wednesdays, and house, electro and rock on Fridays and Saturdays. From 11pm, entrance is only to over 18s on Wednesday and Thursday and over 20s on Friday and Saturday. (☑35 24 52 00; www.rust.dk; Guldbergsgade 8, Nørrebro; ⊙hours vary, club usually 11pm-5am Fri & Sat; ⊟3A, 5A, 350S)

Local Life

### Nørrebro Flea Markets

Nørrebro claims two of Copenhagen's best-loved flea markets. Running every Saturday from early April to the end of October, **Nørrebro Loppemarked** (Map p100, C2; www.berling-samlerting.dk; Nørrebrogade; ⊙8am-3pm Sat, Apr-Oct; ⊟3A, 5A, 350S) takes place along the mustard-coloured wall of Assistens Kirkegård on Nørrebrogade. Turn up early and rummage for offbeat antiques and jewellery, old LPs and the odd Royal Copenhagen Porcelain piece. Four times a year, the street of Ravnsborggade hosts the popular **Ravnsborggade Loppemarked** (Map p100, E3; www.ravnsborggade.dk; Ravnsborggade; ⊙10am-4pm Sun, four times annually; ⊟3A, 5A, 350S), a Sunday affair packed with antiques, retro design and threads. Check the website for dates.

## Local Life
## Østerbro

### Getting There

🚌 **Bus** Route 1A connects central Copenhagen to Trianglen, the heart of Østerbro. From Vesterbro and Nørrebro, route 3A also reaches Trianglen.

Detractors might call it 'white bread' and boring, but salubrious Østerbro serves up some satisfying urban surprises, including heritage-listed architecture and a cinema-turned-design Valhalla. The neighbourhood's name means 'East Gate', a reference to the city's old eastern entrance. These days it's an area best known for its resident media stars, academics and slew of foreign embassies.

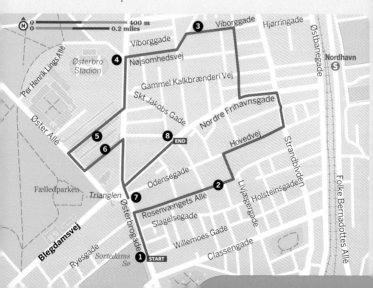

## ❶ Sortedams Sø

Sortedams Sø (Black Dam Lake) is the most northerly of Copenhagen's trio of central lakes. It's popular with joggers and flâneurs, and a good spot to sit and reflect.

## ❷ Rosenvænget

Bordered by Rosenvængets Sideallé, Strandboulevarden, Holsteinsgade and Nordre Frihavnsgade, Rosenvænget is the city's oldest suburban development, established in the mid-19th-century. Rosenvængets Allé 46 was designed by Vilhelm Dahlerup, creator of Ny Carlsberg Glyptotek.

## ❸ Pixie

Light-strung, boho cafe-bar **Pixie** (www.cafepixie.dk; Løgstørgade 2; dishes Dkr55-179; ⊙8am-midnight Mon-Thu, to 4am Fri & Sat, 10am-11pm Sun) looks straight off the streets of Buenos Aires. If the weather's on your side, grab a table on the leafy square, order a latte, and take in the giant wooden fruit sculptures beside you.

## ❹ Øbro-Hallen

Inspired by the baths of ancient Rome, beautiful **Øbro-Hallen** (www. kulturogfritid.kk.dk/øbro-hallen; Gunnar Nu Hansens Plads 3; adult Dkr35, child weekdays/weekends Dkr16/5; ⊙7am-8pm Mon, Tue & Thu, 10am-8pm Wed, 7am-9pm Fri, 9am-3pm Sat & Sun) is Denmark's oldest indoor public pool complex (1929–30). It's also one of its most beautiful, awash with natural light from its elegant glass ceiling.

## ❺ Brumleby

Celebrated Danish writers Martin Andersen Nexø *(Pelle the Conqueror)* and Peter Høeg *(Miss Smilla's Feeling for Snow)* have both called Brumleby home. A heritage-listed combo of yellow-and-white row-housing and cosy gardens, the residential enclave was built to better house the poor after the 1853 cholera epidemic.

## ❻ Olufsvej

Technicolour Olufsvej is lined with 19th-century workers' abodes in a multitude of shades. These days, the properties are home to a number of well-known journalists.

## ❼ Normann Copenhagen

Sprawling **Normann Copenhagen** (☎35 27 05 40; www.normann-copenhagen. com; Østerbrogade 70; ⊙10am-6pm Mon-Fri, to 4pm Sat; 🚍1A, 3A, 14) bursts with must-have design objects, from statement bowls and glassware to furniture, lighting and cushions. The space was once a cinema.

## ❽ Fischer

Another reformed local is **Fischer** (☎35 42 39 64; www.hosfischer.dk in Danish; Victor Borges Plads 12, Østerbro; pasta Dkr139, dinner mains Dkr189-235; ⊙11am-10pm Mon-Fri, 10.30am-10pm Sat & Sun; 🚍3A), a former workingman's bar turned neighbourly trattoria. It makes sense that the Italian grub is so good, given that owner and head chef David Fischer worked the kitchen at Rome's Michelin-starred La Pergola.

Explore

# Vesterbro

Once best known for butchers and hookers, Vesterbro is now the epicentre of Copenhagen cool. The neighbourhood's hottest corner remains Kødbyen (Meat City), a still-functioning Meatpacking District pimped with buzzing eateries, bars, galleries, music venues and start-ups. Istedgade mixes porn shops with vintage boutiques and ethnic groceries, while further north lies continental Værnedamsvej.

VIEW PICTURES LTD/ALAMY ©

# The Sights in a Day

☀ Like Nørrebro, Vesterbro is more about the vibe than blockbuster tourist sights. Start with breakfast or brunch at **Granola** (p108), one of Copenhagen's best-loved cafes. It's right on Værnedamsvej so once you're done, shop-hop the street. Further west on adjoining Vesterbrogade is **Designer Zoo** (p117), a solid spot for local design.

☀ When the hunger pangs hit, lunch on beautiful Danish grub at **Øl & Brød** (p113), then sneak in a cheeky craft beer at neighbouring **Mikkeller** (p116). Continue south along Viktoriagade to Istedgade, where you could easily spend the rest of the afternoon hunting down vintage threads and quirky knick-knacks or just kicking back at a cafe for a spot of people watching.

☾ Continue south to the post-industrial cool of Kødbyen for drinks and dinner. Top eating choices here include **Kødbyens Fiskebar** (p113) and **Nose2Tail** (p115). If you feel like hanging around, jump into **Mesteren & Lærlingen** (p117) or **Bakken** (p116), or head back to the western end of Istedgade, off which lies **Vega** (p117), Copenhagen's legendary live music and club venue.

For a local's day in Vesterbro, see p110.

## 🔍 Local Life

Continental Værnedamsvej (p110)

## 💜 Best of Copenhagen

**Eating**
Kødbyens Fiskebar (p113)

Øl & Brød (p113)

Pony (p115)

**Drinking**
Falernum (p109)

Lidkoeb (p116)

Mikkeller (p116)

## Getting There

🚆 **S-Train** Central Station lies at the eastern end of Istedgade, from where Kødbyen is an easy walk southwest.

🚌 **Bus** Routes 6A and 26 run along Vesterbrogade, while route 9A travels along Gammel Kongevej one block north. Routes 10 and 14 run along Istedgade; these two latter routes are also convenient for Kødbyen.

## Local Life
# Continental Værnedamsvej

Copenhageners have a soft spot for Værnedamsvej, a sassy little strip they commonly compare to the side streets of Paris. Gallic or not, it is one of Vesterbro's most appealing pockets, dotted with specialist cheese and wine shops, cafes and bistros, petite boutiques and an unmistakably easy, local vibe. Some shops close on the weekends, so head in during the week for the full experience.

**1** Granola

Arguably the most famous of Værnedamsvej's residents, **Granola** (☏40 82 41 20; Værndemsvej 5, Vesterbro; lunch Dkr75-145, dinner mains Dkr135-195; ☉7am-10pm Mon-Fri, 9am-10pm Sat, 9am-4pm Sun; ☐6A, 9A, 26) is a staple of Copenhagen's breakfast and weekend brunch scene. The look is a little 'old-school general store',

and the food fresh and flavour packed. If it's AM, tuck into the fruit-laced oatmeal or pancakes. If it's PM, fill up on the *moules marinière* or braised pork.

### 2 Juuls Vin og Spiritus

Vintage wine shop **Juuls Vin og Spiritus** (www.juuls.dk; Værnedamsvej 15; ⊙9am-5.30pm Mon-Thu, to 7pm Fri, to 2pm Sat; ☐6A, 9A, 26) sells some thirst-inducing drops, not to mention an impressive range of whiskys. Fine local choices include spicy, fruity Brøndum Kummenaquavit, as well as organic snaps from Hven, a tiny Swedish island located in the Øresund.

### 3 Falernum

Worn floorboards and chairs, bottle-lined shelves and soothing tunes give wine bar **Falernum** (☎33 22 30 89; www.falernum.dk; Værnedamsvej 16; ⊙noon-midnight Sun-Thu, to 2am Fri & Sat; 🛜; ☐6A, 9A, 26) a deliciously moody air. You'll find around 40 wines by the glass alone, as well as boutique beers, coffee and a simple, seasonal menu of sharing plates like osso buco with roasted artichokes and onions, as well as cheeses and charcuterie.

### 4 Dora

Christian Lacroix notebooks, quilted laptop covers, hand-painted lava-stone cheese: design shop **Dora** (www.shopdora.dk; Værnedamsvej 6; ⊙10am-6pm Mon-Fri, to 4pm Sat, noon-4pm Sun; ☐6A, 9A, 26) likes to keep things highly idiosyncratic, with harder-to-find objects for any room and any occasion. Look out for cool local stuff from brands like Hay and LuckyBoySunday.

### 5 Playtype

Font freaks will go gaga at **Playtype** (www.playtype.com; Værnedamsvej 6; ⊙noon-6pm Mon-Fri, 10am-4pm Sat; ☐6A, 9A, 26), an online type foundry with its own real-life, hard-copy shop. The theme is Danish-designed fonts, showcased as letters, numbers and symbols on everything from posters, notebooks and postcards to crew necks, raincoats, laptop covers and mugs.

### 6 Prag

Just around the corner from Værnedamsvej is **Prag** (www.pragcopenhagen.com; Vesterbrogade 98A; ⊙10am-6pm Mon-Fri, to 5pm Sat; ☐3A, 6A). It's one of Copenhagen's funkiest consignment stores, peddling an eclectic booty of threads and accessories for both women and men. Need a frou-frou frock or tutu? A polka-dot bow tie? Maybe a vintage kimono? Chances are you'll find it here.

### 7 Just Spotted

If you're after unique souvenirs, **Just Spotted** (www.justspotted.dk; Oehlenschlægersgade 13; ⊙noon-5pm Mon-Fri; ☐6A) stocks Copenhagen-themed posters from artists like KLAM, Sivellink, Martin Moore, Hamide and Wonderhagen. Many of the posters have a classic, modernist feel and prices are reasonable.

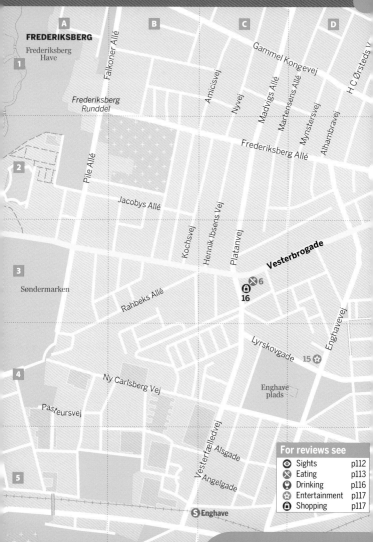

FREDERIKSBERG

Frederiksberg
Have

Frederiksberg
Runddel

Falkoner Allé

Gammel Kongevej

Amicisvej

Nyvej

Madvigs Allé

Martensens Allé

Mynstersvej

Alhambravej

H C Ørsteds v

Frederiksberg Allé

Pile Allé

Jacobys Allé

Kochsvej

Henrik Ibsens Vej

Platanvej

**Vesterbrogade**

Søndermarken

Rahbeks Allé

6
16

Lyrskovgade

Enghavevej

15

Ny Carlsberg Vej

Enghave
plads

Pasteursvej

Vesterfælledvej

Alsgade

Angelgade

Enghave

E

F

G

H

1

Skt Knuds Vej

Vodroffsvej

Vester Søgade

Nyropsgade

Vester Farimagsgade

Hammerichsgade

*Sankt Jørgens Sø*

**Vesterport** Ⓢ

*Imax Tycho Brahe Planetarium* ◉1

Ved Vesterport

Frederiksberg Allé

Værnedamsvej

**Vesterbrogade**

Helgolandsgade

2

Ⓟ11

**Central Station (Københavns Hovedbanegård)**

Ⓢ

Reventlowsgade

Colbjørnsensgade

5 ✖

Ⓟ
10

Viktoriagade

Gasværksvej

3

Matthæusgade

Eskildsgade

Absalonsgade

Tietgensgade
◉2

*DGI-byen*

Ingerslevsgade

Istedgade

Dannebrogsgade

Skydebanegade
13

✖8

✖9

7
4
✖

12
Ⓟ

*Flæsketorvet*

*V1 Gallery*
◉3

4

Saxogade

Sønder Blvd

Skelbækgade

Kødbyen (Meatpacking District)

14

Valdemarsgade

Flensborggade

Dybbølsgade

Ingerslevsgade

Ⓢ**Dybbølsbro**

5

Ⓝ 0 —————— 500 m
0 —————— 0.25 miles

# Sights

## Imax Tycho Brahe Planetarium
PLANETARIUM

1 🎯 Map p110, G2

Explore the heavens at Copenhagen's planetarium, with its state-of-the-art equipment capable of projecting more than 7500 stars, planets and galaxies in its domed Space Theatre. The centre also screens IMAX and 3D/4D films on subjects ranging from sea monsters to Irish rockers U2. While the films are narrated in Danish, English-language headphones (Dkr20) are available at the ticket counter. (☑ 33 12 12 24; www.tycho.dk; Gammel Kongevej 10; adult/child Dkr144/94; ⏱ noon-7.40pm Mon, 10.45am-7.40pm Tue-Thu & Sun, 10.45am-8.50pm Fri & Sat; 🚌 9A, 🚉 S-train Vesterport)

> Q Local Life
> ## Cykelslangen
> Designed by local architects Dissing + Weitling, the bright-orange Cykelslangen is an elevated 235m-long cycling path that winds its way from Bryggebro (Brygge Bridge) west to Fisketorvet Shopping Centre. Extending out over the harbour, it offers one of Copenhagen's most thrilling bike rides. To reach the path on public transport, catch bus 30 to Fisketorvet Shopping Centre. The best way to reach it, however, is on a bike, as Cykelslangen is only accessible to cyclists.

## DGI-byen
POOL, GYM

2 🎯 Map p110, H3

An extravagant indoor swim centre with several pools, including a grand ellipse-shaped affair with 100m lanes, a deep 'mountain pool' with a climbing wall, a hot-water pool and a children's pool. If you've forgotten your togs or towels, they can be hired for Dkr25 each (bring photo ID as a deposit). There's also a small gym on the premises. (www.dgi-byen.dk; Tietgensgade 65; day pass adult/child Dkr65/45, day pass before 9am Mon-Fri Dkr45/30; ⏱ 6.30am-10pm Mon-Thu, 6.30am-7.30pm Fri, 9am-7pm Sat, 9am-6pm Sun; ♿; 🚌 1A, 820, 🚉 København H)

## V1 Gallery
GALLERY

3 🎯 Map p110, H4

Part of the Kødbyen (Vesterbro's 'Meatpacking District'), V1 is one of Copenhagen's most progressive art galleries. Cast your eye on fresh work from both emerging and established local and foreign artists. Some of the world's hottest names in street and graffiti art have exhibited here, from Britain's Banksy to the USA's Todd James and Lydia Fong (aka Barry McGee). (☑ 33 31 03 21; www.v1gallery.com; Flæsketorvet 69-71; admission free; ⏱ noon-6pm Wed-Fri, to 4pm Sat during exhibitions; 🚌 10, 14)

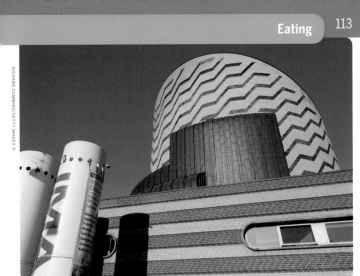

RICHARD CUMMINS/GETTY IMAGES ©

Imax Tycho Brahe Planetarium designed by architect Knud Munk

# Eating

## Kødbyens Fiskebar    SEAFOOD $$$

4  Map p110, G4

Concrete floors, industrial tiling and a 1000L aquarium meets impeccable seafood at this Michelin-listed must, slap bang in Vesterbro's trendy Kødbyen ('Meat City' district). Ditch the mains for three or four starters; the oysters are phenomenal, while the silky razor clams, served on a crisp, rice-paper 'shell', are sublime. You can book a table, but dining at the Manhattan-style bar is much more fun. (☏32 15 56 56; fiskebaren.dk; Flæsketorvet 100; mains Dkr215-255; ⏱5.30-11pm daily; ☐10, 14)

## Øl & Brød    DANISH $$

5  Map p110, G2

Modernist Danish furniture, Arne Jacobsen cutlery and a muted palette of greys and greens offer the perfect backdrop to high-end, contemporary smørrebrod. Decide between the five- or seven-course menu (the latter includes matching craft beers) and raise your glass to sophisticated re-inventions like dried and smoked goose breast with soft-boiled egg, stewed corn and chervil. The restaurant claims Denmark's largest collection of akavit and snaps. (☏33 31 44 22; www.mikkeller.dk/ol-brod; Viktoriagade 6; 5/7-course menu Dkr500/1100;

Understand

## Sustainable Capital

While some Western governments continue to debate the veracity of climate-change science, the Danish capital gets on with sustainable business. The result is one of the world's most environmentally enlightened urban centres.

### Windy Ambitions

Wind power generates around 30% of Denmark's energy supply, with a government target of 50% by 2020. The country is a market leader in wind-power technology, with Danish companies having installed over 90% of the world's offshore wind turbines to date. The long-term goal for Danish energy policy is clear: the entire energy supply – electricity, heating, industry and transport – is to be powered by renewable energy by 2050. Copenhagen has set itself the target of becoming the world's first carbon-neutral capital by 2025.

### On Your Bike

Copenhagen has made cycling an integral part of its urban planning and design. On the busiest commuter routes, so-called 'Green Waves' see green traffic lights coordinated with 'waves' of cyclists. The result is a smooth, nonstop journey for those peddling at the average speed of 20km/h. The city offers more than 400km of safe, continuous bike paths. It's a network being constantly improved and expanded. A recent addition is the spectacular Cykelslangen (p112), an elevated bike track that meanders over the harbour. Impressively, 52% of all Copenhageners now commute daily by bike.

### Harbour Rehab

Less than two decades ago, Copenhagen's inner waterways were littered with algae, sewage, industrial waste and oil spills. The degradation propelled the city council to activate a long-term recovery plan. The sewer system was modernised and treatment plants upgraded. In 1995, 93 overflow channels pumped waste water into the city's harbour and surrounding coast, a problem greatly reduced with the construction of rainwater reservoirs and reservoir conduits able to hold waste water until the sewage system frees up. The result is a revitalised, swimmable harbourfront.

⏱11.30am-10pm Tue-Thu & Sun, to 11pm Fri & Sat; 🚌6A, 10, 14, 26, 🚆S-train København H)

## Pony

MODERN DANISH $$

6 ✖ Map p110, C3

If your accountant forbids dinner at Kadeau (p78), opt for its bistro spin-off, Pony. While the New Nordic grub here is simpler, it's no less stunning, with palate-punching marvels like tartar with black trumpet mushrooms, blackberries and mushroom broth, or lemon sole with cauliflower, pickled apples, kale, almonds and capers. The vibe is convivial and intimate. Book ahead, especially on Friday and Saturday. (☎33 22 10 00; www.ponykbh. dk; Vesterbrogade 135; dishes Dkr110-185, 4-course menu Dkr450; ⏱5.30-10pm Tue-Sun; 🚌6A)

## Nose2Tail

DANISH $$

7 ✖ Map p110, G4

Finding its muse in the Danish bars of yesteryear, this basement factory-turned-noshery uses every part of the animal to cook up honest, rustic fare served on wooden chopping blocks. The menu is short and seasonal, the produce mainly local and organic, and the vibe equally cool and cosy – think candlelight flickering on white industrial tiles, old Danish crockery and crooked old photos. (☎33 93 50 45; Flæsketorvet 13; mains Dkr150-190; ⏱6-10pm Mon-Thu, to 11pm Fri & Sat; 🚌10, 14)

## Paté Paté

INTERNATIONAL $$

8 ✖ Map p110, G4

Another Kødbyen favourite, this pâté factory-turned-restaurant/wine bar gives Euro classics modern twists. While the menu changes regularly, signature dishes include refreshing burrata (a fresh Italian cheese made from mozzarella and cream) with roasted peach, pesto, chilli and browned butter, and earthy grilled piglet with mojo rojo (a chilli-based sauce), *sobrasada* (raw cured sausage), borlotti beans and grilled carrots. It's hip and bustling, yet utterly convivial; bonus extras include clued-in staff, a well-versed wine list and solo-diner-friendly bar seating. (☎39 69 55 57; www.patepate.dk; Slagterboderne 1; dishes Dkr80-130; ⏱9am-10pm Mon-Thu, 9am-11pm Fri, 11am-11pm Sat; 📶; 🚌10, 14)

## Mother

PIZZERIA $$

9 ✖ Map p110, G4

Pizzeria Mother ditches gingham tablecloths for sexy concrete floors, industrial tiles and an X-factor Kødbyen address. The bubbling, thin-crust pie is made with organic sourdough and topped with real-deal ingredients like buffalo mozzarella and prosciutto di Norcia. If there's a wait for a table (likely), pull up a log at Mother's adjoining bar and down an Aperol Spritz. (www.mother.dk; Høker-boderne 9-15; pizzas Dkr75-145; ⏱8am-11pm Mon-Fri, 11am-11pm Sat, 11am-10pm Sun; 📶; 🚌10, 14)

# Drinking

## Mikkeller

BAR

10 Map p110, G3

Low-slung lights, moss-green floors and 20 brews on tap: cult-status Mikkeller flies the flag for craft beer, its rotating cast of suds including Mikkeller's own acclaimed creations and guest drops from microbreweries from around the globe. The bottled offerings are equally inspired, with cheese and snacks to soak up the foamy goodness. (www.mikkeller.dk; Viktoriagade 8B-C; 1pm-1am Sun-Wed, to 2am Thu & Fri, noon-2am Sat; ; 6A, 10, 14, 26, S-train København H)

### Local Life

#### Dyrehaven

Once a spit-and-sawdust working-class bar (the vinyl booths and easy-wipe floors tell the story), **Dyrehaven** (Map p110, E5; www.dyrehavenkbh.dk; Sønder Blvd 72; breakfast Dkr28-120, lunch Dkr58-85, dinner mains Dkr125-162; 9am-midnight Mon-Wed, to 2am Thu & Fri, 10am-2am Sat, 10am-midnight Sun, kitchen closes 9pm Sun-Thu, 10pm Fri & Sat; ; 1A, 10, 14) is now a second home for Vesterbro's cool, young bohemians. Squeeze into your skinny jeans and join them for cheap drinks, simple tasty grub (the 'Kartoffelmad' egg open sandwich is a classic, made with homemade mayo and fried shallots) and some late-night camaraderie.

## Lidkoeb

COCKTAIL BAR

11 Map p110, F2

Lidkoeb loves a game of hide and seek: follow the 'Lidkoeb' signs into the second, light-strung courtyard. Once found, this top-tier cocktail lounge rewards with passionate barkeeps and clever, seasonal libations. Slip into a Børge Mogensen chair and toast to Danish ingenuity with Nordic bar bites and drinks like the Koldskål: a vodka-based twist on Denmark's iconic buttermilk dessert. Extras include a dedicated upstairs whisky bar with over 100 drops. ( 33 11 20 10; www.lidkoeb.dk; Vesterbrogade 72B; 4pm-2am Mon-Sat, 8pm-1am Sun; ; 6A, 26)

## Bakken

BAR

12 Map p110, G4

Affordable drinks, DJ-spun disco and rock, and a Meatpacking District address make intimate, gritty Bakken a magnet for attitude-free hipsters. (Flæsketorvet 19-21; 6pm-4am Fri & Sat; 10, 14)

## Sort Kaffe & Vinyl

CAFE

13 Map p110, F4

This skinny little cafe/record store combo is a second home for Vesterbro's coffee cognoscenti. Join them for velvety espresso, hunt down that limited edition Blaxploitation LP, or score a prized pavement seat and eye-up the eye-candy regulars. ( 61 70 33 49; Syydebanegade 4; 8am-7pm Mon-Wed, 8am-10pm Thu & Fri, 9am-10pm Sat, 9am-7pm Sun; 10)

## KBIII
CLUB

**14** 📍 Map p110, G4

KBIII is the biggest club in the kicking Kødbyen district, aptly occupying a giant former meat freezer. Although events span film screenings, live acts, burlesque and release parties, the emphasis is on thumping club tunes from resident and global DJs, with past deck guests including Just Blaze and Secondcity. Come summer, the club's backyard is a buzzing party spot. (📞33 23 45 97; www.kb3.dk; Kødboderne 3; ⏱champagne bar 8pm-late Thu-Sat, club 11pm-4am Fri & Sat; 🚌1A, 🚊S-train to Dybbølsbro)

# Entertainment

## Vega Live
LIVE MUSIC

**15** ⭐ Map p110, D4

The daddy of Copenhagen's live-music and club venues, Vega hosts everyone from big-name rock, pop, blues and jazz acts to underground indie, hip hop and electro up-and-comers. Gigs take place on either the main stage (Store Vega), small stage (Lille Vega) or the revamped ground-floor Ideal Bar. The venue itself is a 1950s former trade union HQ by leading Danish architect Vilhelm Lauritzen. Performance times vary; check the website.

○ Local Life
### Mesteren & Lærlingen

In a previous life, **Mesteren & Lær-lingen** (Map p110, G4; Flæsketorvet 86; ⏱8pm-3am Wed-Sat) was a slaughterhouse bodega. These days it's one of Copenhagen's in-the-know drinking holes, its tiled walls packing in a friendly, hipster crowd of trucker caps and skinny jeans. Squeeze in and knock back a rum and ginger (the house speciality) to DJ-spun retro, soul, reggae and country.

(📞33 25 70 11; www.vega.dk; Enghavevej 40; 📶; 🚌3A, 10, 14)

# Shopping

## Designer Zoo
DESIGN

**16** 🔒 Map p110, C3

If you find yourself in Vesterbro – and you should – make sure to drop into this supercool design complex. Here, fashion, jewellery and furniture designers, as well as ceramic artists and glass blowers, work and sell their limited edition, must-have creations. (📞33 24 94 93; www.dzoo.dk; Vesterbrogade 137; ⏱10am-5.30pm Mon-Thu, to 7pm Fri, to 3pm Sat; 🚌6A)

## Local Life
# Frederiksberg

Copenhageners dream of a Frederiksberg address. Located directly west of Vesterbro, it's a moneyed district, laced with fin-de-siècle architecture, neighbourly bistros and leafy residential streets. It's here that you'll find the landscaped elegance of Frederiksberg Have and the architecturally notable Copenhagen Zoo, as well as one of Copenhagen's finest flea markets.

### Getting There

🚌 **Bus** Route 9A runs past Frederiksberg Rådhus (City Hall). Route 18 runs along the eastern edge of Frederiksberg Have. Route 6A runs along the park's southern flank (including the zoo). Route 26 stops near Carlsberg Brewery.

Ⓜ **Metro** Forum station lies 300m north of Frederiksberg Rådhus.

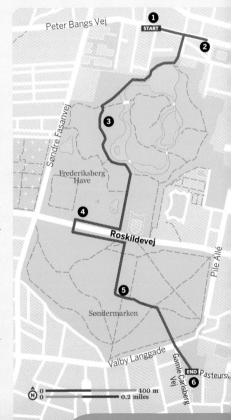

**❶ Sokkelund**

Classic **Sokkelund** (☎38 10 64 00; http://cafe-sokkelund.dk; Smallegade 36E, Frederiksberg; salads Dkr135-165, mains Dkr165-259; ☺8am-10pm Mon-Fri, 9.30am-10pm Sat, 9.30am-9pm Sun; ☏; 🚌9A, 72, 73, Ⓜ Frederiksberg) is the quintessential neighbourhood brasserie, kitted out with leather banquettes, newspapers on hooks and handsome waiters in crisp white shirts. Breakfast, lunch or dinner, join the steady stream of regulars for flexible bistro bites, including some of the juiciest burgers in town.

**❷ Frederiksberg Loppetorv**

If it's Saturday, scour cult-status flea market **Frederiksberg Loppetorv** (Frederiksberg Flea Market; Smallegade, Frederiksberg Rådhus; ☺8am-3pm Sun mid-Apr–mid-Oct; 🚌9A, 18, 71, 72, 73, 74). The neighbourhood's affluence is reflected in the quality of the goods, and seasoned treasure hunters head in early for the best finds. There's usually plenty of local and international fashion, with the odd Danish design collectable in the mix.

**❸ Frederiksberg Have**

Romantic **Frederiksberg Have** (main entrance Frederiksberg Runddel; ☺6am-9pm daily; 🚌18, 26) woos with its lakes and woodlands. Look out for the Chinese summerhouse pavilion, built in 1803 by court architect Andreas Kirkerup. Overlooking the park is Frederiksborg Slot, a former royal palace, now home to the Royal Danish Military Academy.

**❹ Copenhagen Zoo**

Perched on Frederiksberg (Frederik's Hill), **Copenhagen Zoo** (☎72 20 02 00; www.zoo.dk; Roskildevej 32; adult/child Dkr160/95; ☺10am-6pm Jun & Aug, to 8pm Jul, reduced hours rest of year; 🚌4A, 6A, 72) rumbles with more than 2500 of nature's lovelies. Its elephant enclosure was designed by English architect Sir Norman Foster, and the newer Arctic Ring enclosure allows visitors to walk right through the polar-bear pool.

**❺ Cisternerne**

Below Søndermarken Park lurks Copenhagen's 19th-century water reservoir. These days it's best known as **Cisternerne** (www.cisternerne.dk; Søndermarken; adult/child Dkr50/free; ☺11am-5pm Tue-Sun Apr-Nov; 🚌6A, 72), one of Copenhagen's most unusual art spaces. The gallery runs one major exhibition every year – check the website.

**❻ Carlsberg Brewery**

Carlsberg Brewery was designed by architect Vilhelm Dahlerup. The brewery's **visitors centre** (☎33 27 12 82; www.visitcarlsberg.dk; Gamle Carlsberg Vej 11; adult/child Dkr80/60; ☺10am-5pm Tue-Sun; 🚌18, 26) explores the history of Danish beer from 1370 BC, leading you past antique copper vats and the brewery's famous Jutland dray horses. The self-guided tour ends at the bar, where two free beers await. A new visitors centre is due to open in 2017.

## Top Sights
# Louisiana

### Getting There

🚆**S-Train** From Central Station and Nørreport, S-trains run regularly to Humlebæk station. From here, the museum is a 1.5km signposted walk along Gammel Strandvej.

Even if you don't have a consuming passion for modern art, Denmark's outstanding Louisiana should be high on your 'to do' list. It's a striking modernist gallery, located in the town of Humlebæk, 30km north of central Copenhagen, made up of four huge wings, which stretch across a sculpture-filled park, burrowing down into the hillside and nosing out again to wink at the sea (and Sweden).

North Wing, Louisiana

# Don't Miss

## Permanent Collection

The museum's permanent collection, mainly post-war paintings and graphic art, covers everything from constructivism, CoBrA movement artists and minimalist art to abstract expressionism, pop art and staged photography. Pablo Picasso, Francis Bacon and Alberto Giacometti are some of the international luminaries you'll come across inside, while prominent Danish artists include Asger Jorn, Carl-Henning Pedersen, Robert Jacobsen and Richard Mortensen.

## Architecture

The Danish architects Vilhelm Wohlert and Jørgen Bo spent several months walking around the grounds before deciding on their design for Louisiana. The result would be one of the country's finest examples of modernist architecture, a series of horizontal, light-washed buildings in harmony with their natural surroundings. The museum's three original buildings – completed in 1958 and known as the North Wing – are now accompanied by subsequent extensions. The seats in the Concert Hall are the work of the late designer Poul Kjaerholm.

## Sculpture Garden

With views across the deep-blue Øresund to Sweden, Louisiana's arresting grounds are peppered with sculptures from some of the world's most venerated artists. You'll find works from the likes of Max Ernst, Louise Bourgeois, Joan Miró, Henry Moore and Jean Arp, each one positioned to interact with the environment surrounding it. Site-specific works include George Trakas' *Self Passage* and Richard Serra's *The Gate in the Gorge*.

www.louisiana.dk

Gammel Strandvej 13, Humlebæk

adult/child Dkr110/free

🕘 11am-10pm Tue-Fri, to 6pm Sat & Sun

## ☑ Top Tips

▶ Check the museum website for upcoming events, which include regular evening art lectures and live music.

▶ If you have kids in tow, head to the Children's Wing, where they can create their own masterpieces inspired by the gallery's exhibitions.

## ✖ Take a Break

With its large sunny terrace and sea views, Louisiana's cultured cafe is a fabulous spot for lunch or a reviving coffee.

# The Best of
# **Copenhagen**

Søndermarken, Frederiksberg (p118)
KATERYNA NEGODA/GETTY IMAGES ©

# Best Walks
# Scenes from Borgen

## 🏃 The Walk

A cult hit from Reykjavík to Rio, political drama *Borgen* is one of Denmark's best-loved, most critically acclaimed TV series to date. It centres on the Machiavellian world of politics and the media, as well as the very human struggles of those at the top, and one of the show's main stars is the city itself. Relive your favourite small-screen moments on this easy tour of *Borgen*'s most iconic settings.

**Start** Marmorbroen; 🚌11A to Ny Vestergade

**Finish** Cafe Wilder; 🚌2A, 9A, 40 or 350S to Torvegade, Ⓜ to Christianshavn

**Length** 2km; 1.5 hours

## ✗ Take a Break

Wine or dine at protagonist Katrine's own local, Cafe Wilder (p80).

Christiansborg Slot (p36)

### ❶ Marmorbroen

It's on the rococo **Marble Bridge** that soon-to-become prime minister Birgitte Nyborg meets Troels Höxenhaven, who offers to release racist emails written by Nyborg's political opponent, Michael Laugesen.

### ❷ Christiansborg Ridebane

The porticoes of Christiansborg Slot's **Riding Ground Complex** is the setting for many impromptu meetings, including those between Birgitte and her unlikeable coalition partner, Pernille Madsen.

### ❸ Christiansborg Slot Tower

Head into Christiansborg Slot through the main entrance to climb the palace **tower** (p37). It's here that Birgitte's party vice-chairman and mentor Bent Sejrø encourages her to fight for the role of *statsminister*.

### ❹ Det Kongelige Biblioteks Have

The open archways of the red-brick building facing Christiansborg

Slot's southern side lead to the **Royal Library Garden**, where Birgitte confronts Justice Minister, Troels Höxenhaven, about holding a press conference without her knowledge after it's revealed that the Social Solidarity party's headquarters have been bugged. The garden sits on Christian IV's old naval port. The towering fountain sculpture, by Mogens Møller, is an ode to the written word.

**❺ Det Kongelige Bibliotek**

Just south of the garden, Det Kongelige Bibliotek is home to restaurant **Søren K** (p43), where Birgitte meets Labour leader Bjørn Marrot to negotiate the position of EU commissioner in Brussels. The modern office buildings opposite are the studios of the show's fictional TV1.

**❻ Katrine Fønsmark's Apartment**

Head north along the waterfront, cross Knip-pelsbro bridge and turn left into canalside Overgaden Oven Vandet. In the show, No 48 is the **apartment building** in which the ambitious young journalist Katrine Fønsmark lives.

**❼ Cafe Wilder**

Backtrack a few steps to Sankt Annæ Gade, cross the canal, and continue one block to **Cafe Wilder** (p80) where Katrine awkwardly bumps into ex-lover Kasper Juul and his new girlfriend, Lotte.

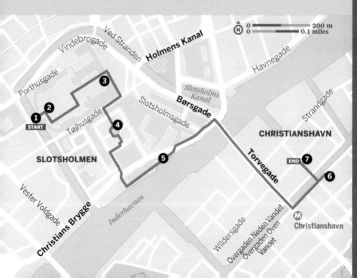

# Best Walks
# **Nørrebro Soul**

## 🏃 The Walk

Nørrebro is Copenhagen's creative heart, a multi-ethnic enclave splashed with quirky parks and street art, intriguing workshops and studios, as well as the city's most beautiful eternal resting place. So tie up those sneakers and hit the pavement for red squares and bulls, giant birds and tankers, and a shady street turned good.

**Start** Superkilen; 🚌5A to Nørrebrogade

**Finish** Jægersborggade; 🚌18 to Jagtvej

**Length** 2km; 1½ hours

## 🍴 Take a Break

End your saunter with superlative coffee at Coffee Collective (p102).

Headstone, Assistens Kirkegård (p101)

### ❶ Superkilen

Created by local architecture studio Bjarke Ingels Group, Berlin-based landscape architects Topotek1 and Danish art group Superflex, the 1km-long park **Superkilen** is a hyperplayful ode to the area's multicultural fabric, with Russian neon signs, Ghanaian bollards and even a Spanish bull.

### ❷ Basco5 Mural

Head east along Mimersgade, turning left into Bragesgade. On the side of No 35 is a **street art mural** by Copenhagen artist Nils Blishen, better known as Basco5. Birds, bearded men and a round, cartoonish style are all trademarks of the artist's work.

### ❸ BaNanna Park

Turn right into Nannasgade and walk 250m to oil-refinery-turned-playground **BaNanna Park**. Its striking gateway is a 14m-high climbing wall, popular with eye-candy locals and open to all (BYO climbing equipment).

## 4 Odinsgade Murals

Step right into Rådmandsgade, left into Mimersgade, and right again into Thorsgade. Two blocks ahead is Odinsgade. The whimsical **mural** on the side of No 17 is by Simon Hjermind Jensen, Anne Sofie Madsen and Claus Frederiksen. The adjacent tanker mural uses existing architectural features to dramatic effect.

## 5 Assistens Kirkegård

At Jagvej, turn right, and continue to hallowed **Assistens Kirkegård** (p101). In 2013 the cemetery created a 75-sq-metre burial plot for the city's homeless, complete with a bronze sculpture by artist Leif Sylvester. Each day, eccentric local Captain Irishman collects flowers for the plot.

## 6 Jægersborggade

Directly opposite Assistens Kirkegård, Jægersborggade is a vibrant hub of craft studios, boutiques and eateries. At No 27, **Inge Vincents Ceramics** creates crinkled handmade vases, cups, bowls and tealight holders, while at No 47, **flacoDesign** is known for sculptural lamps made with sustainable wood.

# Best
# Museums & Galleries

Copenhagen is packed with engaging museums and galleries, from the epic to the eclectic. Together they house a seemingly endless array of cultural treasures, from ancient tomb wares and sacrificial bodies to dazzling swords and jewels, iconic modernist design and envelope-pushing contemporary installations from Denmark and beyond. Strap on some comfy kicks and hit the ground running.

LOUISIANA MUSEUM OF MODERN ART/POUL BUCHARD/BRØNDUM & CO ©

### Plan Your Visit

Many museums and galleries close at least one day a week, usually on Monday. Some stay open late one or more nights a week, often on Wednesday or Thursday. While Nationalmuseet, Statens Museum for Kunst and Davids Samling are always free, some museums – among them Ny Carlsberg Glyptotek and Thorvaldsens Museum – offer free admission once a week, often on Wednesday or Sunday.

### Park Museums

Statens Museum for Kunst, Rosenborg Slot, Davids Samling, Hirschsprung, Statens Naturhistoriske Museum (including Geologisk Museum and Zoologisk Museum) and Cinemateket together form the newly created **Parkmuseerne** (www.parkmuseerne. dk) district. A combination ticket (Dkr195) covers all venues, and includes one fee-incurring temporary exhibition at Statens Museum for Kunst, as well as a cinema ticket at Cinemateket.

## ☑ Top Tips

▶ If you plan on blitzing the museums, consider purchasing the Copenhagen Card (p150), which offers free entry to more than 70 museums and attractions, including Rosenborg Slot, Amalienborg Slot and Ny Carlsberg Glyptotek.

## Best for History

**Nationalmuseet** The country's entire bio under one roof. (p28)

**Amalienborg Slot** Snoop through the rooms of a royal rococo abode. (p64)

**Designmuseum Danmark** Explore the roots and influences of Danish design. (p60)

Amalienborg Slot (p64)

**Rosenborg Slot** Lust after royal bling in Christian IV's Renaissance summer pad. (p84)

**De Kongelige Stalde** An equine affair of carriages, uniforms and riding equipment at the Royal Stables. (p38)

**Tøjhusmuseet** Analyse historical battles at the Royal Danish Arsenal Museum. (p42)

## Best Art Museums

**Statens Museum for Kunst** Denmark's pre-eminent art collection spans medieval to modern. (p88)

**Louisiana** World-class masterpieces with a side of modernist architecture. (p121)

**Ny Carlsberg Glyptotek** Ancient treasures meet French and Danish beauties. (p31)

**Thorvaldsens Museum** Denmark's first museum building and a shrine to the nation's greatest sculptor. (p41)

## Best Lesser-Known Treasures

**Davids Samling** A neoclassical apartment graced with Eastern and Western treasures. (p93)

**Hirschsprung** An elegant repository of 19th- and 20th-century Danish art. (p94)

**Kongernes Lapidarium** Original royal statues in Christian IV's 17th-century brewery. (p42)

**Dansk Jødisk Museum** Jewry heritage in a space designed by starchitect Daniel Libeskind. (p42)

## Best Contemporary Art Galleries

**Kunsthal Charlottenborg** One of Europe's largest venues for modern talent from around the globe. (p64)

**Kunstforeningen GL Strand** A canalside showcase of forward-thinking local and foreign works. (p49)

**Nikolaj Kunsthal** Contemporary art in Copenhagen's third-oldest church. (p49)

**V1 Gallery** Edgy exhibitions in Vesterbro's Meatpacking District. (p112)

**Overgaden** Next-generation artists at a Christianshavn not-for-profit gallery. (p77)

# Best
## Shopping

What Copenhagen's shopping portfolio lacks in size it more than makes up for with quality and individuality. The city is Scandinavia's capital of cool, with no shortage of homegrown must-haves, from progressive fashion to elegant home wares. So if you find the same-same global chains uninspiring, dive into Copenhagen's side streets and respark your spending fire.

### Where to Shop

Global and local chains line much of Copenhagen's main shopping strip, Strøget. Punctuating the strip is Amagertorv, home to major design stores, including Illums Bolighus, Georg Jensen, Royal Copenhagen Porcelain and (just off the square) Hay House. South of Strøget, pedestrianised Strædet is known for its jewellery and antique stores. For hipper Nordic labels and concept stores, shop the area roughly bordered by Strøget, Købmagergade, Kronprinsensgade and Gothersgade. North of Nyhavn, salubrious Bredgade is lined with exclusive art and antiques. For more-affordable bric-a-brac, vintage jewellery and kitschy interior design, scour the shops on Ravnsborggade in Nørrebro or explore Nørrebro Loppemarked, the neighbourhood's seasonal Saturday flea market. Nørrebro is also home to Elmegade and Jægersborggade, two streets pimped with interesting, independent shops. Vesterbro is another good bet for independent fashion designers and homewares, with most of the offerings on and around Istedgade and Værndamsvej.

MERTEN SNIJDERS/GETTY IMAGES ©

### ☑ Top Tips

▶ Non-EU citizens can claim a 25% tax refund on goods as long as they spend a minimum of Dkr300 per shop, in refund-participating shops. Simply get the store to fill in a refund form, then present it, with your receipts, purchases and passport, at the airport upon departure.

### Best for Cool Hunters

**Bruuns Bazaar** Sexy, classic Scandi style for men and women. (p55)

**Han Kjøbenhavn** Beautifully crafted men's threads fusing hipster and heritage aesthetics. (p55)

Illums Bolighus (p55)

**Storm** Harder-to-find labels, accessories and gifts for clued-in guys and girls. (p56)

**Wood Wood** Hip, street-smart threads and accessories from Wood Wood and beyond. (p56)

**Henrik Vibskov** Bold, avant-garde fashion for those who dare to be different. (p56)

## Best Local Souvenirs & Gifts

**Designmuseum Danmark** Cool, design-savvy gifts, from jewellery and wallets to books and textiles. (p60)

**Just Spotted** Striking graphic posters with Copenhagen motifs. (p109)

**Playtype** Dashing Danish fonts on ceramics,

clothes, laptop covers and more. (p109)

**Designer Zoo** An eclectic range of homewares, furniture and threads from independent local designers. (p117)

**Susanne Juul** Distinctive hats and caps from the capital's top milliner. (p69)

## Best for Gluttons

**Torvehallerne KBH** A celebrated food market heaving with local pantry fillers. (p90)

**Coffee Collective** Pick up a few bags of locally roasted coffee blends. (p126)

**Juuls Vin og Spiritus** Stock the cellar with Nordic akvavits, gins and more. (p109)

## Best for Interior Design

**Illums Bolighus** Designer furniture and objects for every room of your home or office. (p55)

**Klassik Moderne Møbelkunst** Classic Danish furniture for moneyed collectors. (p69)

**Hay House** Contemporary furniture, furnishings and gifts from new-school Scandi talent. (p55)

**Stilleben** Contemporary furnishings from emerging, forward-thinking local designers. (p55)

**Le Klint** Elegant Nordic lighting from renowned architects and designers. (p56)

# Best
## Eating

In little over a decade, Copenhagen has gone from dining dowager to culinary darling, with no less than 15 Michelin-starred restaurants – more than any other Scandinavian city. New Nordic cuisine continues to wow food critics and foodies alike, while Danish classics are enjoying resurgent popularity and modern interpretations.

### Old-School Flavours

Reindeer moss and hay-smoked quail eggs may be the norm on New Nordic menus, but traditional Danish tables are a heartier affair. Pork (*flæsk* or *svinekød*) shines in comfort-food favourite *frikadeller*, fried minced-pork meatballs commonly served with boiled potatoes and red cabbage. Equally iconic is the majestic *stjerneskud*. Literally 'shooting star', it's a belt-busting combination of both steamed and fried fish fillets, topped with smoked salmon, shrimp and caviar, and served on buttered bread.

### The Sweet Stuff

Ironically, what is commonly known as a 'Danish pastry' abroad is known to the Danes as a *wienerbrød* (Viennese bread), and nearly every second street corner has a *bageri* (bakery) with different varieties. As legend has it, the naming of the pastry can be traced to a Danish baker who moved to Austria in the 18th century, where he perfected the treats of flaky, butter-laden pastry. True to their collective sweet tooth, Danes eat them for breakfast. Not that Denmark's pastry selection ends there. Other famous treats include *kanelsnegle* (cinnamon snail), a luscious cinnamon scroll sometimes laced with thick, gooey chocolate.

☑ **Top Tips**

▶ Make sure to reserve a table at popular restaurants, especially later in the week. Many of them now offer easy online reservations.

▶ While Copenhageners love to eat out, they are not Mediterraneans, meaning that if you like to eat late, you'll have trouble finding a place to accommodate you after about 10pm.

LONELY PLANET/GETTY IMAGES ©

Veronabrød (Danish bread)

### Best New Nordic Degustations

**Noma** The Holy Grail for international gastronomes. (p78)

**Kadeau** An edgy culinary ode to the island of Bornholm. (p78)

**Kanalen** The scene's next upcoming superstar. (p78)

### Best Midrange Hot Spots

**Höst** New Nordic revelations for modest wallets. (p94)

**Pony** Modern Danish brilliance at Kadeau's simpler spin-off. (p115)

**Manfreds og Vin** Local produce cooked with honesty and whimsy. (p101)

### Best for Smørrebrød

**Schønnemann** Copenhagen's most historic peddler of open sandwiches. (p50)

**Øl & Brød** Contemporary reinterpretations, boutique beers and Denmark's finest akvavit collection. (p113)

**Aamanns Takeaway** Competent modern twists in a busy, trendy bolthole. (p96)

### Best for Weekend Brunch

**Granola** A Vesterbro classic and much-loved weekend hang-out. (p108)

**Bastionen + Løven** Heritage interiors, romantic garden and a satisfying weekend buffet. (p79)

### Best for Date Night

**Clou** Elegance and style meet contemporary culinary brilliance. (p65)

**Orangeriet** Modern Danish in a charming vintage conservatory. (p94)

**Brasserie Granberg** Beautiful French classics and a snug bistro ambience. (p50)

### Best for Seafood

**Kødbyens Fiskebar** Postindustrial cool and the city's best oysters. (p113)

**Oysters & Grill** Plate-licking surf with a side of Nørrebro conviviality. (p101)

# Best
# Drinking

Copenhagen swings with a multitude of drinking options – pocket-sized cafes brewing Third Wave coffee, slinky cocktail dens serving Nordic-inspired cocktails, and trendy beer bars pouring obscure craft brews. The line between cafe, restaurant and bar is often blurred, with many places changing role as the day progresses.

JOHNER IMAGES/GETTY IMAGES ©

### Where to Drink

Vibrant drinking areas include Kødbyen (the Meatpacking District) and Istedgade in Vesterbro; Ravnsborggade, Elmegade and Sankt Hans Torv in Nørrebro; Nansensgade close to Nørreport; and the maze of streets to the north of Strøget, including Pilestræde and especially gay-friendly Studiestræde. Of course, on a sunny day there's always Nyhavn, although there can be a serious risk of encountering a Dixieland jazz band.

## ☑ **Top Tips**

▸ If your thirst is bigger than your bank balance, hit Nørrebro bar Kassen (p103). Loud, fun and popular, the bar serves up the city's best and longest happy-hour cocktail deals.

### Best for Coffee

**Forloren Espresso** Sip specialist coffees while browsing photography tomes. (p67)

**Coffee Collective** A cult-status microroastery brewing ethically sourced beans. (p90)

### Best for Beers

**Mikkeller** Superlative craft beers. (p116)

**Nørrebro Bryghus** An inner-city microbrewery in funky Nørrebro. (p102)

### Best for Cocktails

**1105** Killer martinis in a dark, sophisticated setting. (p52)

**Ruby** Clever, seasonal cocktails in hideaway rooms. (p52)

**Lidkoeb** A secret cocktail and whisky den in Vesterbro. (p116)

**Union Bar** Sip and slurp the Prohibition way just off Nyhavn. (p67)

### Best for Wine

**Ved Stranden 10** Impeccable wines, roaming sommeliers and classic Danish design. (p52)

**Falernum** A staggering choice of wines by the glass and a *hyggelig* (cosy) atmosphere. (p109)

**Bibendum** Another fine, long wine list, and beautiful small dishes. (p97)

# Best
# **Entertainment**

Copenhagen's X-factor fuels its entertainment options. The city is home to thriving live-music and club scenes that span intimate jazz and blues clubs, mega rock venues and secret clubs dropping experimental beats. Blockbuster cultural venues deliver top-tier opera, theatre and dance, while cinemas screen both mainstream and art-house flicks. Note: many nightspots don't get the party started until 11pm or midnight.

## Best for Jazz

**Jazzhouse** Over 200 concerts annually from local and international jazz masters. (p54)

**La Fontaine** A jazz joint famous for its late-night jams. (p54)

## Best for Live Bands

**Vega Live** Three venues in one, serving up an alphabet of genres. (p117)

**Rust** A classic spot for indie rock, pop, hip hop and electronica. (p103)

**Loppen** Alternative rock and punk, hip hop and reggae in grungy Christiania. (p74)

## Best for Clubbing

**Culture Box** In-the-know DJ talent pumping out electronica, house, techno and bass. (p97)

**Sunday** Cult-status club with an anything-goes attitude. (p53)

**KBIII** A Vesterbro mega-club in the Meatpacking District. (p117)

## Best for Performing Arts

**Det Kongelige Teater** Top-tier ballet and opera in Copenhagen's most opulent period theatre. (p67)

**Skuespilhuset** The contemporary home of the Royal Danish Theatre. (p67)

**Operaen** Sterling opera in a state-of-the art harbourside statement (pictured above right), designed by Henning

## ☑ **Top Tips**

▶ Located at the main Tivoli Gardens entrance, **Tivoli Billetcenter** (☎ 33 15 10 12; Vesterbrogade 3; ⊙10am-8pm Mon-Fri, 11am-5pm Sat & Sun) is good for tickets of any kind. Not only does it sell Tivoli performance tickets, but it's also an agent for **Billetnet** (☎ 70 15 65 65; www.billetnet.dk), which sells tickets for concerts and music festivals nationwide.

Larsen Architects. (p80)

## Best for Cinephiles

**Cinemateket** Modern and classic flicks at the Danish Film Institute. (p54)

# Best
# **Hygge**

While it might be a little unusual to call a feeling a city highlight, in the case of Danish *hygge*, we heartily recommend that you grab a piece of the action.

CHRISTER FREDRIKSSON/GETTY IMAGES ©

## Hygge: 101

What is *hygge*? How do you achieve it? And just how does it feel? Light some candles, pour a warming cup of coffee, and read on.

While there is really no equivalent in English, *hygge* loosely refers to a sense of friendly, warm companionship of a kind fostered when Danes gather together in groups of two or more. The participants don't even have to be friends (indeed, you might only have just met), but if the conversation flows – avoiding potentially divisive topics like politics and the best way to pickle a herring – the bonhomie blossoms, and toasts are raised before an open fire (or, at the very least, some candles), you are probably coming close.

### ☑ **Top Tips**

▶ Danish *hygge* reaches fever pitch in December, when twinkling lights, flowing *gløgg* (mulled wine) and Tivoli's famous Christmas market crank up the cosiness and camaraderie.

## Best for Old-School Hygge

**Tivoli Gardens** A spirit-lifting jumble of carnival rides, twinkling lights and old-fashioned magic. (p24)

**Bankeråt** A lovingly worn pub where the animals are stuffed and the toilets irreverent. (p97)

**Dyrehaven** Everything old is cool again at this hipster Vesterbro hang-out. (p116)

**La Glace** Snuggle up with hot tea and a luscious slice of walnut cake. (p50)

## Best for Hip Hygge

**Manfreds og Vin** A snug neighbourhood eatery with beautiful nosh and wine. (p101)

**Øl & Brød** A modern take on classic Danish design, food, beer and hospitality. (p113)

**Ved Stranden 10** A sophisticated wine bar with cosy rooms and thoughtful service. (p52)

**Lidkoeb** Sheepskin, candles and a festive courtyard set a *hyggelig* scene for superlative libations. (p116)

# Best
## For Free

While Copenhagen is hardly a bargain destination, the city does spoil the well-informed with free thrills, including some of its most impressive sights. Some are always free, while others are free on specific days of the week. Best of all the city's compact size means it's easy enough to save money on transport, keeping costs lower and your spirits higher.

FRANK FELL/GETTY IMAGES ©

### Best Always-Free Museums

**Nationalmuseet** Delve into centuries of historical remnants, from ancient coins to modern Danish kitsch. (p28)

**Statens Museum for Kunst** A who's who of Danish and international art. (p88)

**Davids Samling** A dazzling booty of Islamic treasures, and European paintings and applied arts. (p93)

### Best Sometimes-Free Museums

**Ny Carlsberg Glyptotek** From Egyptian tombs to French impressionists, an eclectic cultural hoard that's free on Sundays. (p31)

**Thorvaldsens Museum** Wednesdays are free at this ode to Denmark's greatest sculptor. (p41)

**Hirschsprung** Explore Danish Golden Age artworks sans cash on Wednesdays. (p94)

### Best Free CPH Experiences

**Assistens Kirkegård** Enjoy one-on-one time with some of Denmark's most illustrious historical figures. (p101)

**Islands Brygge Havnebadet** Work it, flaunt it or just get it wet at Copenhagen's hottest harbour pool complex. (p78)

**Christiania** Soak up the sights, sounds and scents of Copenhagen's most unconventional neighbourhood. (p72)

☑ **Top Tips**

▶ **Copenhagen Free Walking Tours** (www.copenhagenfreewalkingtours.dk) depart daily at 11am and 2pm from outside Rådhus. Tours are in English and require a minimum of five people.

▶ Free 90-minute tours of Christianshavn depart at 4pm Friday to Monday from the base of the Bishop Absalon statue on Højbro Plads.

**Christiansborg Slot Tower** The million-dollar view from Copenhagen's tallest tower will cost you nada. (p37)

# Best
# **Tours**

## Best Overview Tours

**Netto-Bådene** (📞32 54 41 02; www.havnerundfart. dk; adult/child Dkr40/15; ⏱tours 2-5 per hour, 10am-7pm Jul & Aug, to 5pm Apr-Jun & Sep-mid-Oct; 👪) The cheapest of Copenhagen's harbour and canal tours, with embarkation points at Holmens Kirke and Nyhavn.

**Canal Tours Copenhagen** (📞32 66 00 00; www.stromma.dk; adult/child/family Dkr75/35/190; ⏱9.30am-9pm late Jun-late Aug, reduced hours rest of year; 👪) Highly popular one-hour harbour and canal tours departing from Nyhavn and Ved Stranden.

**Copenhagen City Sightseeing** (📞32 66 00 00; www.citysightseeing. dk; ⏱departures every 30-60min, 9.30am-6pm daily, mid-May–mid-Sep, shorter hours & routes rest of year) A hop-on, hop-off bus with three routes to choose from. The two-day 'Bus & Boat combo'

also covers Canal Tours Copenhagen.

## Best Active Tours

**Kayak Republic** (📞30 49 86 20; www.kayakrepublic.dk; Børskaj 12; per person Dkr150-575 ; ⏱10am-8pm) Two-hour and full-day kayak tours along the city's canals, as well as kayak rental for self-exploration. Located just beside Christian IV's Bro.

**Bike Copenhagen With Mike** (📞26 39 56 88; www. bikecopenhagenwithmike. dk; Sankt Peders Stræde 47; per person Dkr299) Idiosyncratic three-hour cycling tours of Copenhagen, departing from Sankt Peders Stræde 47 in the city centre. Seasonal options include a Saturday evening 'Ride & Dine' tour from June to September.

**Running Tours Copenhagen** (📞50 86 95 04; www.runningtours.dk; 1-2 people Dkr375, 3/4 people Dkr560/670) Run or jog your way through the city and its history. Themes include Grand Tour, Night

CHRIS HEPBURN/GETTY IMAGES ©

Tour and Pub Run, with tours commencing in Rådhuspladsen.

## Best Themed Tours

**Nordic Noir Tours** (www. nordicnoirtours.com; per person Dkr150, if booked online Dkr100; ⏱Borgen tour 2pm Sat, The Killing/ The Bridge tour 4pm Sat) Retrace the steps of your favourite Nordic TV characters from *Borgen*, *The Bridge* and *The Killing* on these 90-minute location walking tours. Tours commence from Vesterport S-train station.

**CPH:cool** (📞29 80 10 40; www.cphcool.dk; Vesterbrogade 4A) Two-hour in-the-know walking tours with themes like gastronomy, shopping, architecture and design. Tours leave from outside the Copenhagen Visitors Centre.

 Best
**For Kids**

If the sheer thought of a city break with young kids has you reaching for the Valium, Copenhagen has the solution. The Danish capital seems tailor-made for little ones. And we're not just talking about Northern Europe's biggest aquarium or its most famous amusement park either. We're talking about free entry for kids at most museums, engaging cultural institutions, child-friendly parks and beaches, and a transport system that's pram-friendly.

### Best for Sunny Days

**Tivoli Gardens** Kids' shows, as well as rides that span the tame to the insane. (pictured top right; p24)

**Copenhagen Zoo** Share the pool with polar bears at the zoo's spectacular new Arctic Ring enclosure. (p119)

**GoBoat** Enjoy a picnic on your very own solar-powered boat. (p77)

**Islands Brygge Havnebadet** Safe, clean harbour swimming for kids young and old. (p78)

**Rundetårn** Climb Christian IV's stoic tower for a game of 'spot the city landmarks'. (p48)

**Kongens Have** Run amok beside a fairy-tale castle or catch an outdoor puppet show. (p87)

### Best for Rainy Days

**Nationalmuseet** Sail a ship or be a knight in the National Museum's interactive Children's Museum. (p28)

**DGI-byen** Get soaked the fun way at Copenhagen's top indoor pool complex, complete with 'mountain' and hot pools. (p112)

**Statens Museum for Kunst** Kids' exhibitions and activities nurture budding artists at the National Gallery. (p88)

### ☑ Top Tips

▶ The city's official tourism website www.visitcopenhagen.com has pages dedicated to family holidays – lists of kid-approved attractions, child-friendly restaurants, ace playgrounds in the capital and much more.

**Imax Tycho Brahe Planetarium** Starry skies and Imax films await at Copenhagen's educational planetarium. (p112)

**Louisiana** A world-class museum with its own children's wing. (p121)

# Best
# Architecture

Copenhagen's architectural cache is rich and eclectic, spanning many centuries and architectural styles. Despite its age, the Danish capital bursts with contemporary verve and edge, its Renaissance, baroque and National Romantic treasures sharing the spotlight with modernist icons and innovative just-built marvels.

221A/GETTY IMAGES ©

### Historical Overview

Copenhagen's architectural legacy begins with Bishop Absalon's 12th-century fortress, its ruins visible beneath neobaroque Christiansborg Slot. 'Builder King' Christian IV embarked on an extraordinary building program in the 17th century, its legacy including Børsen, Rundetårn, Rosenborg Slot and Christian IV's Bryghus (home to Kongernes Lapidarium). Rococo delights include Amalienborg Slot and Marmorkirken, while a standout example of the National Romantic style – inspired by Scandinavian heritage and popular at the turn of last century – is Copenhagen's Rådhus (City Hall).

**☑ Top Tips**

▶ Located on Christianshavn, the Dansk Arkitektur Centre (p77) hosts exhibitions on architecture and runs architecture-themed walking tours of the city. See the website for details.

**Rosenborg Slot** A petite castle built in the Dutch Renaissance style. (p84)

**Christiansborg Slot** Copenhagen's biggest, boldest neobaroque statement. (p36)

**Rundetårn** Christian IV's astronomical tower, complete with equestrian staircase. (p48)

**Børsen** A Dutch Renaissance stock exchange with rooftop dragons. (pictured above; p43)

**Marmorkirken** Copenhagen's most dashing rococo show-off. (p64)

**Det Kongelige Bibliotek** The Royal Library's 'Black Diamond' extension heralded a new era for Copenhagen's waterfront. (p41)

**Operaen** Copenhagen's harbourfront opera house divides opinion. (p80)

# Best
## Design

Is there a more design-conscious nation than Denmark, or a more design-obsessed capital than Copenhagen? Sure, the Italians like a nice sofa and the French have their frocks, but in Denmark design excellence runs deeper than that. From its restaurant and hotel interiors to its cycling overpasses, one of Copenhagen's most inspirational qualities is its love and mastery of the applied arts.

### Kaare Klint: Danish Design Pioneer

While modern Danish design bloomed in the 1950s, its roots are firmly planted in the 1920s and the work of pioneering Danish modernist Kaare Klint (1888–1954). The architect spent much of his career studying the human form and modified a number of chair designs for added functionality. Klint's obsession with functionality, accessibility and attention to detail would ultimately drive and define Denmark's mid-20th-century design scene and its broader design legacy.

**Klassik Moderne Møbelkunst** A retail repository for the country's most celebrated chairs, tables and more. (p69)

**Hay House** Furniture, homewares and gifts from new-school Nordic talent. (p55)

**Illums Bolighus** All the biggest names in design on four inspiring levels. (pictured above; p55)

**Höst** The urban-rustic interior of this New Nordic nosh spot has swagged international awards. (p94)

LONELY PLANET/GETTY IMAGES ©

### ☑ Top Tips

▶ For an overview of Denmark's design legacy, visit Design-museum Danmark (p60), a treasure trove of classic Danish pieces. The museum is also home to a notable gift shop.

**Normann Copenhagen**
This converted cinema is now a showcase for modern industrial design. (p105)

# Best
# Festivals & Events

Bass-thumping block parties and saxy jazz, pot-stirring celebrity chefs, groundbreaking films and documentaries, and a rainbow-coloured Pride parade: Copenhagen's social calendar is a soul-stirring, toe-tapping creature. Sunshine, sleet or snow, you're bound to find a reason to head out and celebrate the finer things in life.

HENRIK SØRENSEN/GETTY IMAGES ©

## Best for Culture Vultures

**Art Copenhagen** (www.artcopenhagen.dk) A major three-day art fair in September.

**Kulturnatten** (Culture Night; www.kulturnatten.dk) Late-night art and culture, usually on the second Friday in October.

**Kulturhavn** (www.kulturhavn.dk) Three days of mostly free harbourside events in early August.

## Best for Music

**Copenhagen Jazz Festival** (www.jazz.dk) Copenhagen's biggest festival delivers 10 days of world-class jazz.

**Copenhagen Blues Festival** (www.copenhagen-bluesfestival.dk) Five days of international blues in

late September or early October.

**Strøm** (www.stromcph.dk) A week-long electronic music festival in August.

**Copenhagen 'Distortion'** (www.cphdistortion.dk) Five heady days of club and block parties in early June.

## Best for Foodies

**Copenhagen Cooking** (www.copenhagencooking.dk) Scandinavia's largest food festival runs in August, with a winter edition in February.

## Best for Film Buffs

**CPH:PIX** (www.cphpix.dk) Copenhagen's feature film festival runs for two weeks in April.

**CPH:DOX** (www.cphdox.dk) An acclaimed docu-

mentary film festival running in November.

## Best LGBT Festivals

**Copenhagen Pride** (www.copenhagenpride.dk) LGBT special events and a Pride parade in August.

**Mix Copenhagen** (www.mixcopenhagen.dk) Ten days of local and foreign LGBT films in October.

☑ **Top Tips**

▶ The best sources of up-to-date info on events are www.aok.dk and www.visitcopenhagen.com. Also useful is the English-language *Copenhagen Post* (www.cphpost.dk).

# Best
# **Outdoor Experiences**

Determined to be completely $CO_2$ neutral by 2025, Copenhagen is already one of the world's greenest, cleanest cities. Over 50% of Copenhageners commute by bike on a daily basis, and the city's inner harbour is usually clean enough for a bracing summertime dip. Whether you're after a lazy paddle along the canals, or a picnic in the park, Denmark's enlightened capital has you covered.

G. JORGENSHAUS/GETTY IMAGES ©

## Best Green Escapes

**Kongens Have** Copenhagen's oldest park comes with a castle and puppet theatre. (p87)

**Botanisk Have** Romantic trails and Denmark's most comprehensive collection of plants. (p93)

**Assistens Kirkegård** Amble or picnic in Copenhagen's most famous graveyard. (p101)

**Christiania** Christiania's lesser-trampled corners combine bucolic bliss and architectural ingenuity. (p72)

**Frederiksberg Have** A sprawling, English-style garden that inspired Paul Gauguin. (p119)

## Best Blue Escapes

**Islands Brygge Havnebadet** Copenhagen's see-and-be-seen outdoor harbour pool complex. (p78)

**GoBoat** Nosh, slosh and sail around the city on your own partly recycled boat. (p77)

**Kayak Republic** Take a slow tour of town with a paddle in your hands. (p138)

## Best Alfresco Hang-Outs

**Christiianshavns Bådudlejning & Café**

☑ **Top Tips**

▶ With well over 400km of dedicated cycling paths, Copenhagen is one of the world's greatest cities to experience on a bike.

▶ For cycling tips and clear, detailed information on cycling safety, make sure to check out www.cycleguide.dk.

A floating cafe, bar and boat-hire joint right on a Christianshavn canal. (p80)

**Bastionen + Løven** Lazy weekend brunching in a country garden setting. (p79)

Det Kongeliege Bibliotek's 'Black Diamond' extension (p41), designed by schmidt hammer lassen architects

# Survival Guide

# Survival Guide

# Before You Go

## When to Go

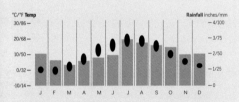

°C/°F Temp
30/86 —
20/68 —
10/50 —
0/32 —
-10/14 —

Rainfall inches/mm
— 4/100
— 3/75
— 2/50
— 1/25
— 0

J F M A M J J A S O N D

➡ **Winter (Dec–Feb)**
Short days and frigid temperatures. Christmas lights, markets and *gløgg* (mulled wine) keep spirits up in December.

➡ **Spring (Mar–May)**
Milder weather usually arrives around April. Outdoor attractions begin to reopen.

➡ **Summer (Jun–Aug)**
The best time to visit, with long daylight hours and plenty of outdoor festivals and events.

➡ **Autumn (Sep–Nov)**
Crisp days and brilliant bursts of red and gold illuminate the city's parks. November heralds the winter gloom.

## Book Your Stay

☑ **Top Tip** The rates of some hostels and most midrange and top-end hotels are based on supply and demand, with daily fluctuations. In most cases, booking early guarantees the best deal.

➡ It's a good idea to book in advance – rooms in many of the most popular midrange hotels fill quickly, particularly during the convention season, typically from August to October.

➡ Copenhagen's hostels often fill early in summer so it's best to make reservations in advance. You will need a hostelling card to get the advertised rates at hostels belonging to the Danhostel organisation.

➡ You can book rooms in private homes (Dkr350/500 for singles/doubles); there is a Dkr100 booking fee if you do it via the tourist office when you arrive, otherwise it is free online.

➔ The tourist office also books unfilled hotel rooms at discounted rates of up to 50% (sometimes even more). These discounts, however, are based on supply and demand.

### Useful Websites

**Lonely Planet** (www.lonelyplanet.com/hotels) Author-reviewed accommodation and online booking.

**Booking.com** (www.booking.com) Online hotel search engine and booking service.

**Airbnb** (www.airbnb.com.au)

**Visit Copenhagen** (www.visitcopenhagen.com) Copenhagen's official tourism website, with hotel, B&B and apartment reviews and online booking.

### Best Budget

**Generator Hostel** (www.generatorhostel.com) Upbeat, buzzing, design-literate hostel on the very edge of the city's medieval core. Bathrooms in both dorms and private rooms.

**Wakeup Copenhagen** (www.wakeupcopenhagen.com) Book early for true budget rates at this simple, stylish hotel. There are two locations, one near Central Station, the other near Nyhavn.

### Best Midrange

**Hotel Guldsmeden** (www.hotelguldsmeden.com) There are four Guldsmeden boutique hotels in town, each featuring Balinese-inspired chic, organic breakfasts and beautiful service.

**Hotel Alexandra** (www.hotelalexandra.dk) Very central and recently renovated, with attentive staff and effortlessly cool rooms decked out in mid-century Danish style.

### Best Top End

**Hotel d'Angleterre** (www.dangleterre.com) Copenhagen's most glamorous slumber palace. Plush rooms and suites deliver contemporary twists on classic luxury. Indoor pool and spa.

**Nimb Hotel** (www.nimb.dk) Luxurious, design-savvy boutique hotel right by Tivoli. All but three rooms feature a fireplace, while all bar one overlook Tivoli Gardens.

# Arriving in Copenhagen

☑ **Top Tip** For the best way to get to your accommodation, see p17.

## Copenhagen Airport

**Copenhagen Airport** (CPH; www.cph.dk) CPH is located 9km southeast of central Copenhagen. Terminal 1 is for domestic flights, and Terminals 2 and 3 for international flights.

**Metro** (www.m.dk) Runs every four to 20 minutes between the airport (Lufthavnen) and city. It does not stop at Central Station (Københavns Hovedbanegård, commonly known as København H) but is handy for Christianshavn and Nyhavn. Journey time to Kongens Nytorv (stop for Nyhavn) is 14 minutes (Dkr36).

**S-Train** (www.dsb.dk) Connects the airport to Copenhagen Central Station around every 12 minutes. Journey time is 14 minutes (Dkr36).

**Taxi** Expect to pay between Dkr250 and

Dkr300 to the city centre. Travel time is about 20 minutes, depending on traffic.

## Søndre Frihavn

Søndre Frihavn is situated 2km north of central Copenhagen and serves ferries to and from Oslo, Norway. From Central Station, catch the S-train to Nordhavn station, from where the port is a 10- to 15-minute walk. Bus 26 connects the port to many parts of the city.

# Getting Around

Plan your trip using the very handy www.rejseplanen.dk. Copenhagen's compact size, reliable public transport and bike-friendly roads make driving largely unnecessary.

## Bicycle

☑ **Best for...** Flexibility and experiencing the city like a local.

➡ Copenhagen vies with Amsterdam as the world's most bike-friendly city, with dedicated cycling lanes on most streets and state-of-the-art city bikes (p48).

➡ Bike rental outlets include Baisikeli in Vesterbro and Københavns Cyklerbørs near Botanisk Have (Botanical Garden).

➡ Bikes can be carried free on S-trains, but not at Nørreport station during weekday peak hours. Enter carriages through the middle door. Bikes can be carried on the metro (except from 7am to 9am and from 3.30pm to 5.30pm on weekdays from September to May). Bike tickets cost Dkr13.

## Bus

☑ **Best for...** Crossing larger distances in the city, such as Nyhavn to Vesterbro.

➡ **Movia** (www.moviatrafik.dk) runs seven primary routes, each with the letter 'A' in the route number. These routes run every three to seven minutes in peak hour, and about every 10 minutes at other times.

➡ Night buses (denoted by an 'N' in the route number) run on a few major routes between 1am and 5am nightly.

## Metro

☑ **Best for...** Quick commuting between Nørreport, Kongens Nytorv and Christianshavn, and for reaching the airport.

➡ The metro consists of two lines: M1 (green) and M2 (yellow).

➡ Services run 24 hours, every two to four minutes in peak times, three to six minutes during the day and on weekends, and seven to 20 minutes at night.

➡ A city circle line (Cityringen) is due for completion in late 2018 or early 2019.

## S-Train

☑ **Best for...** Sights further afield, including Louisiana modern art museum.

➡ Copenhagen's suburban train network (S-tog in Danish) runs seven lines through Central Station (København H). Other useful inner-city stations are Nørreport and Østerbro.

➡ The network covers a number of popular tourist towns, including Helsingør.

➡ Services run every four to 20 minutes from approximately 5am to

## Tickets & Passes

Copenhagen's bus, metro, S-train (S-tog) and harbour bus (commuter ferry) network has an integrated ticket system based on seven geographical zones. Most of your travel within the city will be within two zones. Travel between the city and airport covers three zones.

The cheapest single ticket (billet) covers two zones, offers unlimited transfers and is valid for one hour (adult Dkr24, 12 to 15 years Dkr12). Children under 12 travel free if accompanied by an adult.

More convenient is the Rejsekort – a smart card that covers all zones and all public transport across the country. It costs Dkr180 (Dkr80 for the card and Dkr100 in credit) and can be bought and topped-up from Rejsekort machines at metro stations, Central Station or the airport.

To use, tap the Rejsekort against the dedicated sensors at train and metro stations or when boarding buses and commuter ferries, then tap off when exiting. Only tap off at the very end of your journey – if your journey involves a metro ride followed immediately by a bus ride, tap on at the metro station and again on the bus, but only tap off once you exit the bus.

If you plan on blitzing the sights, the tourist-saver includes free public transport.

12.30am. All-night services run hourly on Friday and Saturday (half-hourly on line F).

## Harbour Bus

☑ **Best for...** A cheap harbour cruise and commuting between waterfront sights, such as Operaen and the Royal Library.

**Movia** (www.moviatrafik. dk) runs commuter ferries (known as Harbour Buses), with three routes servicing 10 stops. Useful stops for visitors include Det Kongelige Bibliotek (Royal Library), Nyhavn and Opera.

## Taxi

☑ **Best for...** Door-to-door commuting, especially for longer distances and late at night.

➡ Taxis can be flagged on the street and at ranks around the city centre. If the yellow taxa (taxi) sign is lit, the taxi is available for hire.

➡ The fare starts at Dkr37 (Dkr50 from 11pm to 7am Friday and Saturday) and costs Dkr14.20 per km from 7am to 4pm Monday to Friday and Dkr18.75 from 11pm to 7am Friday and Saturday. The rate at all other times is Dkr15.

➡ Most taxis accept major credit cards. The main companies include **DanTaxi** (☎70 25 25 25; www.dantaxi.dk), **Taxa** (☎35 35 35 35; www.taxa.dk) and **Amager-Øbro Taxi** (☎27 27 27 27; www.amagerobro taxi.dk).

# Essential Information

## Business Hours

Standard business hours are as follows:

**Banks** 10am-4pm weekdays (until 5pm or 5.30pm on Thursday)

**Bars** 4pm-midnight, to 2am or later Friday & Saturday (clubs on weekends may open until 5am)

**Cafes** 8am-5pm or midnight

**Restaurants** noon-10pm (maybe earlier on weekends for brunch)

**Shops** 10am-6pm weekdays (often until 7pm on Friday), to 4pm Saturday; some larger stores open Sunday

**Supermarkets** 8am-9pm (often until 8pm or earlier on weekends)

## Discount Cards

**Copenhagen Card** (www. copenhagencard.com; adult/ child 10-15 24hr Dkr339/179, 48hr Dkr469/239, 72hr Dkr559/289), available at the visitors centre or online, gives you free access to 72 museums and attractions in the city and surrounding area, as well as free travel for all S-train, metro, bus and harbour bus journeys within the seven travel zones.

## Emergency

**Ambulance, Fire & Police** (☎112)

## Electricity

230V/50Hz

## Money

### Currency

Denmark's currency is the krone. One krone is divided into 100 øre. There are 50 øre, Dkr1, Dkr2, Dkr5, Dkr10 and Dkr20 coins. Notes come in denominations of 50, 100, 200, 500 and 1000 kroner.

### ATMs

Most banks in Denmark have 24-hour ATMs that give cash advances on Visa and MasterCard credit cards as well as Cirrus and Plus bank cards.

## Credit Cards

Credit cards such as Visa and MasterCard are widely accepted in Denmark (American Express and Diners Club less so). In many places a surcharge may be imposed on foreign cards (up to 3.75%).

## Public Holidays

**New Year's Day** (Nytårsdag) 1 January

**Maundy Thursday** (Skærtorsdag) Thursday before Easter

**Good Friday** (Langfredag) Friday before Easter

**Easter Day** (Påskedag) Sunday in March or April

**Easter Monday** (2.påskedag) Day after Easter

**Great Prayer Day** (Stor Bededag) Fourth Friday after Easter

**Ascension Day** (Kristi Himmelfartsdag) Sixth Thursday after Easter

**Whitsunday** (Pinsedag) Seventh Sunday after Easter

**Whitmonday** (2.pinse dag) Seventh Monday after Easter

**Constitution Day** (Grundlovsdag) 5 June

**Christmas Eve** (Juleaften) 24 December (from noon)

**Christmas Day** (Juledag) 25 December

**Boxing Day** (2.juledag) 26 December

**New Year's Eve** (Nytårsaften) 31 December (from noon)

## Telephone

### Mobile Phones

☑ **Top Tip** If you're coming from outside Europe, check that your phone will work in Europe's GSM 900/1800 network (US phones work on a different frequency).

➜ The cheapest and most practical way to make calls at local rates is to purchase a Danish SIM card and pop it into your own mobile phone. Make sure that your phone isn't blocked from doing this by your home network.

➜ You can buy and top-up a prepaid SIM card at supermarkets, post offices, kiosks and petrol stations throughout the country.

### Useful Numbers

**Local Directory Assistance** (☎118)

**International Directory Assistance** (☎113)

## Money-Saving Tips

➜ Several museums offer free entry, either daily or once weekly (p137).

➜ Seniors and students qualify for discounts on some transport fares and museum entry fees, but you'll need to show proof of student status or age.

➜ Self-catering at supermarkets and markets can help keep food costs down.

➜ Consider getting around on foot – compact Copenhagen was made for walking.

## Tourist Information

**Copenhagen Visitors Centre** (Map p30; ☎70 22 24 42; www.visitcopenhagen. com; Vesterbrogade 4A; ⏱9am-6pm Mon-Sat, to 2pm Sun May, Jun & Sep, 9am-7pm Jul & Aug, 9am-4pm Mon-Fri, to 2pm Sat Oct-Apr; 🛜) Copenhagen's excellent information centre offers free maps and brochures, booking services and a hotel reservations service.

## Travellers with Disabilities

☑ **Top Top** In the 'Special Travel' section under 'Practical Information', the official www.visitdenmark. com website has a useful series of links for travellers with disabilities and explains how to access detailed information.

➜ Copenhagen is improving access for travellers

with disabilities, although accessibility is still not ubiquitous. Major sights are usually well-equipped.

➜ A useful resource is **God Adgang** (www. godadgang.dk), which lists service providers who have had their facilities registered and labelled for accessibility.

## Visas

➜ No entry visa is needed by citizens of EU and Nordic countries.

➜ Citizens of the USA, Canada, Australia and New Zealand need a valid passport to enter Denmark, but they don't need a visa for tourist stays of less than 90 days. The Danish Immigration Service publishes a list of countries whose citizens require a visa at www. nyidanmark.dk.

# Language

Most of the sounds in Danish have equivalents in English, and by reading our pronunciation guides as if they were English, you're sure to be understood. There are short and long versions of each vowel, and additional 'combined vowels' or diphthongs. Consonants can be 'swallowed' and even omitted completely, creating (together with vowels) a glottal stop or *stød* steudh which sounds rather like the Cockney pronunciation of the 'tt' in 'bottle'. Note that *ai* is pronounced as in 'aisle', *aw* as in 'saw', *eu* as the 'u' in 'nurse', *ew* as the 'ee' in 'see' with rounded lips, *ow* as in 'how', *dh* as the 'th' in 'that', and *r* is trilled. The stressed syllables are in italics in our pronunciation guides. Polite and informal forms are indicated with 'pol' and 'inf' respectively.

To enhance your trip with a phrasebook, visit **lonelyplanet.com**.

## Basics

**Hello.**
*Goddag.* — go·*da*

**Goodbye.**
*Farvel.* — faar·*vel*

**Yes./No.**
*Ja./Nej.* — ya/nai

**Please.**
*Vær så venlig.* — ver saw *ven*·lee

**Thank you.**
*Tak.* — taak

**You're welcome.**
*Selv tak.* — sel taak

**Excuse me.**
*Undskyld mig.* — awn·skewl mai

**Sorry.**
*Undskyld.* — awn·skewl

**How are you?**
*Hvordan går det?* — vor·*dan* gawr dey

**Good, thanks.**
*Godt, tak.* — got taak

**What's your name?**
*Hvad hedder* — va *hey*·dha
*De/du?* (pol/inf) — dee/doo

**My name is ...**
*Mit navn er ...* — mit nown ir ...

**Do you speak English?**
*Taler De/du* — ta·la dee/doo
*engelsk?* (pol/inf) — eng·elsk

**I don't understand.**
*Jeg forstår ikke.* — yai for·*stawr* i·ke

## Eating & Drinking

**What would you recommend?**
*Hvad kan De/du* — va kan dee/doo
*anbefale?* (pol/inf) — an·bey·fa·le

**Do you have vegetarian food?**
*Har I* — haar ee
*vegetarmad?* — vey·ge·*taar*·madh

**Cheers!**
*Skål!* — skawl

**I'd like (the) ..., please.**
*Jeg vil gerne* — yai vil *gir*·ne
*have ..., tak.* — ha ... taak

  **bill**
  *regningen* — *rai*·ning·en

  **drink list**
  *vinkortet* — veen·kor·tet

  **menu**
  *menuen* — me·*new*·en

## Emergencies

**Help!**
*Hjælp!* — yelp

**Go away!**
*Gå væk!* — gaw vek

**Call ...!**
*Ring efter ...!* — ring ef·ta ...

   **a doctor**
   *en læge* — in le·ye

   **the police**
   *politiet* — poh·lee·tee·et

**It's an emergency!**
*Det er et* — dey ir it
*nødstilfælde!* — neudhs·til·fe·le

**I'm lost.**
*Jeg er faret vild.* — yai ir faa·ret veel

**I'm sick.**
*Jeg er syg.* — yai ir sew

**It hurts here.**
*Det gør ondt her.* — dey geur awnt heyr

**I'm allergic to...**
*Jeg er allergisk* — yai ir a·ler·geesk
*over for...* — o·va for...

**Where's the toilet?**
*Hvor er toilettet?* — vor ir toy·le·tet

## Shopping & Services

**I'm looking for ...**
*Jeg leder efter ...* — yai li·dha ef·ta ...

**How much is it?**
*Hvor meget* — vor maa·yet
*koster det?* — kos·ta dey

**Can I have a look?**
*Må jeg se?* — maw yai sey

## Time & Numbers

**What time is it?**
*Hvad er klokken?* — va ir klo·ken

| | | |
|---|---|---|
| **1** | *en* | in |
| **2** | *to* | toh |
| **3** | *tre* | trey |
| **4** | *fire* | feer |
| **5** | *fem* | fem |
| **6** | *seks* | seks |
| **7** | *syv* | sew |
| **8** | *otte* | aw·te |
| **9** | *ni* | nee |
| **10** | *ti* | tee |
| **100** | *hundrede* | hoon·re·dhe |
| **1000** | *tusind* | too·sen |

## Transport & Directions

**Where's the ...?**
*Hvor er ...?* — vor ir ...

**What's the address?**
*Hvad er adressen?* — va ir a·draa·sen

**How do I get there?**
*Hvordan kommer* — vor·dan ko·ma
*jeg derhen?* — yai deyr·hen

**Please take me to (this address).**
*Vær venlig at* — ver ven·lee at
*køre mig* — keu·re mai
*til (denne adresse).* — til (de·ne a·draa·se)

**Please stop here.**
*Venligst stop her.* — ven·leest stop heyr

| | | |
|---|---|---|
| **boat** | *båden* | baw·dhen |
| **bus** | *bussen* | boo·sen |
| **plane** | *flyet* | flew·et |
| **train** | *toget* | taw·et |

# Behind the Scenes

## Send Us Your Feedback

We love to hear from travellers – your comments help make our books better. We read every word, and we guarantee that your feedback goes straight to the authors. Visit **lonelyplanet.com/contact** to submit your updates and suggestions.

Note: We may edit, reproduce and incorporate your comments in Lonely Planet products such as guidebooks, websites and digital products, so let us know if you don't want your comments reproduced or your name acknowledged. For a copy of our privacy policy visit lonelyplanet.com/privacy.

## Our Readers

Thanks to the travellers who used the last edition and wrote to us with helpful hints, useful advice and interesting anecdotes:

Holly Atkinson, Andrew Lang, Patrik Leu, Ann Falck Nordskar, Kevin van Schie

## Cristian's Thanks

*Tusind tak* to Martin Kalhoj, Christian Struckmann Irgens, Mette Cecilie Perle Smedegaard, Grete Seidler, Mia Hjorth Lunde, Jens Lunde, Henrik Lorentsen, Gitte Kærsgaard, Henrik Sieverts Ørvad, Brian Jakobsen and René Ørum for their insights and generosity. Thanks also to my diligent colleague and friend Carolyn Bain.

## Acknowledgments

Cover photograph: Central Copenhagen, Andreas Gradin/Alamy

## This Book

This 3rd edition of Lonely Planet's *Pocket Copenhagen* was written by Cristian Bonetto. The previous edition was written by Cristian Bonetto and Michael Booth. This guidebook was produced by the following:

**Destination Editor** Gemma Graham **Product Editor** Martine Power **Senior Cartographer** Valentina Kremenchutskaya **Book Designer** Mazzy Prinsep **Assisting Editors** Imogen Bannister, Justin Flynn, Gabrielle Stefanos **Assisting Book Designer** Wendy Wright **Cover Researcher** Naomi Parker **Thanks to** Sasha Baskett, Penny Cordner, Brendan Dempsey, Ryan Evans, Larissa Frost, Claire Naylor, Karyn Noble, Ellie Simpson, Lyahna Spencer, Angela Tinson, Lauren Wellicome

# Index

# Our Writer

### Cristian Bonetto

According to Cristian Bonetto, Copenhagen is the ultimate modern metropolis: at once compact and cosmopolitan, cool and cosy, historic and at the cutting-edge. The city's knack for fresh ideas provides an endless source of inspiration for the confessed air-miles-hoarder, who has been writing passionately about Danish lamps, bikes and bites for almost a decade. Indeed, the Australian-born writer has contributed to almost 20 Lonely Planet titles to date, including *Denmark*, *Scandinavia*, *Italy*, *New York City* and *Singapore*. Beyond Lonely Planet, his musings on travel and trends have featured everywhere from Britain's *Telegraph* and *BBC Travel*, to San Francisco's *7x7* and Dubai Eye 103.8's The Travel Show. You can follow Cristian's latest adventures on Twitter (@CristianBonetto) and on Instagram (rexcat75).

**Published by Lonely Planet Publications Pty Ltd**
ABN 36 005 607 983
3rd edition – Apr 2015
ISBN 978 1 74220 034 7
© Lonely Planet 2015  Photographs © as indicated 2015
10 9 8 7 6 5 4 3 2 1
Printed in China